FIORENZA

Simonetta

by

Fay Picardi

Burnt Umber Press
2015

Simonetta by Fay Picardi
Book design and Cover: Kathy Garvey and Fay Picardi

Also by Fay Picardi:
Kentucky Poems
Copyright © 2000 Fay Picardi
        (private press)
Nana's Sunday Dance
Copyright © 2010, 2011 Fay Picardi
Second edition: Copyright © 2014 Fay Picardi
        Burnt Umber Press
The Stones Speak
Poetry by Fay Picardi and Art by Cindy Michaud
Copyright © 2011 Cindy Michaud and Fay Picardi
        Burnt Umber Press

Burnt Umber Press
Melbourne, FL

This book is dedicated to Barbara Holmstrup Holly, an extraordinary scholar, teacher and poet. She was my dear friend whose wisdom and humor enriched my life for over forty years. Her editing of the first three chapters of this book before her death in December of 2013 has directly influenced my writing and revision of the whole of this work.

Preface

Simonetta Vespucci arrived in Florence at the age of fifteen during the height of the Italian Renaissance. She had recently been married to Marco Vespucci, also fifteen, the son of a successful Florentine merchant and diplomat. Within a year, poets, politicians and historians alike were writing of her beauty and grace. As her reputation grew, she was also praised for her superior qualities of gentle spirit, intellect and goodness. Even today she remains the image of the ideal woman, remembered primarily for her physical beauty as portrayed in the paintings of Botticelli.

The Florence which Simonetta encountered for the first time in 1469 was extravagant and complex. For the sixty years between 1434 when Cosimo de' Medici the Elder became de facto head of the Republic of Florence and 1494 when his grandson Lorenzo il Magnifico died, the Medici led the city and its territories in an unparalleled era of economic, artistic and scholarly excellence. The Republic of Florence enjoyed unimaginable wealth as the mercantile and banking center of Europe. Its artists and architects including Leonardo da Vinci, Michelangelo, Botticelli and Brunelleschi were among the most talented the world has ever known. The Platonic Academy or Accademia, founded by Cosimo and continued by Lorenzo, included the best scholars, linguists, philosophers, poets, and artists of the time. The Accademia had many experts in the translation and study of Greek and Latin classics, in particular those of Plato. Their work had a profound influence on the beginnings of Humanistic thinking.

As euphoric as this period sounds, these years were not without problems. There were outside threats from France, Spain, the Kingdom of Naples and even the Papacy itself. Internal discontent, political ambitions and threats of rebellions or assassinations were constantly present. The Medici were forced to maintain a relentless vigilance to evade these threats. Both Cosimo the Elder and Piero, his son, had dealt with multiple foreign invaders and personal assassination threats. However, the victims of the assassination plot that was to have the most profound impact on the history of Florence were Lorenzo de' Medici and his brother Giuliano. Lorenzo was the political head of Florence at the time, but Giuliano was the more popular with the citizens. Therefore, the assassins contrived to kill both brothers at the same time in order to assure that the Medici dynasty could not continue. This scheme is known as the Pazzi Conspiracy. The increasingly horrifying nightmares which Simonetta experiences in this narrative are based on historical accounts of this conspiracy.

Often referred to during her lifetime as La Bella Simonetta, La Bella or simply Simonetta, this extraordinary young woman remains an enigma. Despite her renown, her classical education, and her intimacy with the Medici and the Accademia, the only official documents that can be found pertaining to her are the record of her marriage contract with Marco Vespucci in August of 1468 and the annotation of her death. No letters, journals or diaries written by her have survived.

The primary sources of information about Simonetta can be found in the writings of her contemporaries who have recorded their personal acquaintance with her or their observations of her. They were prominent scholars, members of the Accademia, artists and poets. Among Lorenzo de' Medici's prolific writings are many passages and poems written directly about Simonetta. Others, including Giuliano de' Medici, wrote poems about her. The most notable among these poems is the epic *Stanzas Begun on the Tournament of the Magnificent Giuliano de' Medici* written by Angelo Poliziano.

Today, Simonetta Vespucci's naked image as painted by Sandro Botticelli in his *Birth of Venus* can be found on almost every street corner and in almost every shop window in Florence. If Helen of Troy's face launched a thousand ships, Botticelli's depiction of Simonetta has unleashed a frenzy of artistic reproductions and parodies which appear on such items as mugs, scarves, ties, pencil holders and notebooks. Even Andy Warhol was unable to resist creating his own version of the face of Botticelli's *Venus*.

Although few people know Simonetta Vespucci's name, her physical attributes and feminine allure are instantly recognizable. Through the years, she has been lauded by many. Still, little is known about the personal life of this young woman. In researching and writing this biography, I have tried to recreate the person she may have been. I hope I have done her justice.

Author's Notes

This narrative is divided into five parts, each representing a single day between April 18 and April 27 of 1476. Each is introduced by a historical quotation.

*

The paintings of Sandro Botticelli figure prominently in the narrative. Although the artist does not appear in the book until Chapter 16, the descriptions of Simonetta's clothing, jewelry and hair decorations are taken directly from Botticelli's paintings or the banner he executed for the tournament of Giuliano. Many of the scenes Simonetta imagines and the mythical characters she evokes in her dreams were inspired by these paintings.

*

The translations of the writings of Lorenzo de' Medici, Piero Vespucci, Angelo Poliziano and others are my own. Except as noted, all letters, dreams, reminiscences and conversations are my invention. The servants and merchants, including Consolata, are based on readings about households of the period. All other names presented in the book are historically accurate.

*

The details of everyday life including food and drink, clothing and furniture in addition to utilitarian and precious objects such as jewelry are based on accounts, histories, journals and/or artifacts from this time period. The Medici palaces and villas are described as they existed in the 15th century. The Vespucci palace is based loosely on the Davanzati Palazzo in Florence, now a museum of Renaissance architecture and furnishings. Simonetta's room closely resembles the Lady's Bedroom in that museum.

Chronology

1449   Lorenzo de' Medici is born.

1453   Simonetta Cattaneo, Marco Vespucci and Giuliano de' Medici are born.

1464   Cosimo de' Medici the Elder dies. Piero, his son, is appointed de facto head of the Republic of Florence.

1468   Simonetta Cattaneo and Marco Vespucci are betrothed and celebrate their marriage at Piombino.

1469   Simonetta and Marco journey to Florence and celebrate their marriage at the Vespucci palace on Borgo Ognissanti.

1469   The grand tournament of Lorenzo de' Medici is held.

1469   Lorenzo de' Medici and Clarice Orsini wed.

1469   Piero de' Medici dies. Lorenzo de' Medici, his son, is installed as de facto head of the Republic.

1472   Simonetta's half sister, Battistina, and her husband, Jacopo Appiani III, are poisoned at Piombino.

1473   Alfonso, heir to the throne of Naples, arrives in Florence for the grand ball of Eleanora d'Aragona.

1474   The Papacy transfers its banking interests from the Medici to the Pazzi.

1475   Giuliano de' Medici's tournament is given by Lorenzo.

1476   Giuliano and Lorenzo de' Medici depart for Pisa on April 8.

1476   The events of this narrative occur between April 18 and April 27.

1478   The Pazzi Conspiracy is perpetrated.

Simonetta

(There lived) in our city a young woman who touched the hearts of all the Florentine people, which is no surprise for she was gifted a beauty and gentleness of spirit which surpassed all others who had ever lived. Among her many other qualities, her manner was so sweet and bounteous that all who knew her believed themselves to be loved by her. Young men and women of her own age did not envy her excellence and virtue. Rather they praised and exalted her beauty and goodness in such a way that it was impossible to believe that so many men could love her without jealousy and so many women could praise her without envy.

From *Il commento dei miei sonetti* by Lorenzo de' Medici

Part I

18 April 1476

Most esteemed and honorable Lorenzo:

... La Simonetta is still in the same condition that she was when you left and little has gotten better. We are waiting for M. Stefano as we would for any man of such diligence, and thus we hope he will do what must be done.

Your devoted servant, Piero Vespucci
18 April 1476, Florence

Simonetta Cattaneo Vespucci suddenly sits bolt upright in her bed, her bedclothes soaking wet from the kind of cold sweat that only fear can bring. She is staring in disbelief at what she perceives to be the glint of a dagger illuminated by a beam of light which has worked its way from between the slats of the wooden shutters into obscurity at the foot of her bed. Instinct compels her to close her eyes and stiffen her body. Without thinking she claps her hand over her mouth to suppress the scream that is trying to erupt from her.

When she opens her eyes again, Simonetta sees the point of the weapon plunge downward. This time there is no stopping the pitiful sound that escapes her. She can only pray that no one has heard it. After a few seconds, she pulls the bed coverings up around her shoulders and tries to quiet her trembling.

As Simonetta struggles to force the vision of her most recent nightmare from her mind, her body relaxes a bit and the tremors becomes less violent. Then, without warning, she begins to cough in ragged bursts as if she were trying to rid herself of some horrid poison.

Dear Mother of God, never have I needed your comfort as I need it now. Every night I am tormented by the same ordeal. The horror is always the same. The dream is always the same.

As I accompany the Vespucci family to Il Duomo for high Mass on Easter, the early morning streets of Florence are already full of vendors. When we walk into the square before the cathedral, I am surprised by the sunlight sparkling on the marble of the San Giovanni Baptistery. Its undulating movement on the burnished bronze of Ghiberti's Gates of Paradise *captivates me. I watch the shadows move across the doors and onto the faces of the saints standing so solemnly against the facade of the cathedral opposite. Light and form interplay around me. How grateful I am that I can see the beauty of God's world almost as if I were an artist.*

Once Piero has opened the heavy wooden doors of Santa Maria del Fiore, the family enters Il Duomo. I wait at the rear for my eyes to adjust to the darkness. Each time the interior seems more of a mystery. A single shaft of light passes through the stained-glass oculus of the dome's eastern drum. The light filters through the Madonna's skirt, mingles with the dust motes that surround the choir like morning fog rising from a river, and creates a luminescence that makes the altar appear to be floating in space.

Once my eyes become accustomed to the dimness, I walk forward, kneel, make the sign of the cross and join the others in the family pew, taking my place beside Piero, as he would have me do. Holding my body very still, I wait for the Mass to begin. My mind will not be held still. It hangs suspended like the dust motes I have just seen before me, continually moving and trying to catch the light.

Just after the bell rings for the elevation of the Host, I see in the recesses of the cathedral to the left of the altar what seems to be an apparition, the face of my beloved. Then one isolated movement in the enormity of the apse. The thrust of a dagger. I recoil. My fear is as great as if this same dagger were being held over my own head. I hunch my shoulders to receive the blow.

Then I am in my own bed again.

Mother of God, what fear do I harbor, or even worse, what sin am I hiding from myself that causes me to be haunted by this recurring dream? Each morning I try to force myself awake from this nightmare. Each morning the same dagger hangs suspended aloft over the foot of my bed. I am forced to acknowledge the awful glint of it and its terrifying thrust downward. In my dream and in my awakening, I can never completely rid myself of the horror of this one vision. I pray, Mother of God, please beseech your Son to take this torment from me. Amen.

Desperate to distract herself from the despair which she is feeling, Simonetta looks about her, then at the tall casement windows with their sinuous arches which provide the whole room with brightness all year long and in summer, a cool breeze from the mountains to the east.

For more than seven years now I have awakened here on Via Borgo Ognissanti in this room which overlooks the Arno as it begins to descend toward the sea on the western edge of Florence. This bed with its satin covers, velvet quilts and feather mattresses piled so high I nearly disappear into their softness has been my refuge. How is it possible all these years have passed? Only a few weeks ago I celebrated my twenty-third birthday.

Carefully, Simonetta pulls back the covers and swings her legs over the bed. Without making the least sound, she places her bare feet on the wooden step and stands up. Although she has not rid herself completely of the image of the dagger, she knows what she needs to do. Still shivering a little, she sets her feet into the slippers Consolata, her Consi, has left for her and gingerly steps down onto the cold terracotta tiles.

From the foot of the bed, Simonetta picks up the peacock morning robe she uses to shake off the chill she feels even in summer before the sun rounds the southern window. Without waiting for the cloth to warm her, she crosses the floor to the broad window opposite her bed, mounts the stone steps, and throws back the shutters. As the soft sunlight fills the room, she begins to feel her strength returning.

How I do love this room. In this room I can even think kindly of Piero. When I look at the heavy mahogany nuptial bed he had carved for our wedding gift, I have no doubt his intentions as a father-in-law were honorable, and I chide myself for my constant suspicions of his motives. The bed's simplicity, the single carved flowering vine that curves up each of the four bedposts and around the entire cornice board at the top, has never failed to please me. Lying abed, I often trace the soft waxed edge of the vine with my moistened fingertips.

24

But my wedding chest, my very own special cassone that sweet, sweet Gaspi, my dearest father, had carved and painted for me in Genoa, is what I love most of all. Thank you, dear mother, now so far away, for insisting that the painting on the front be a portrait of Venus as she arrives in Portovenere, the sea lapping around her and the wind blowing her long golden hair in great shocks of beauty, and not a biblical scene or a great battle, as is customary. Each time the townspeople retell the story of her arrival, it becomes more and more embellished until Venus no longer comes ashore in a skiff, but floating on a shining sea shell, attended by Zephyr and the goddesses, Aura and Hora. I have heard the myth repeated so many times it has become a part of me, or I a part of it.

As Simonetta glances from the cassone which sits beside the bed across the room to the Tabernacle mirror above her writing table, her face suddenly has the slightest tinge of pink. Her Giuli, Giuliano de' Medici, gave her this treasure. On the right side of the mirror's intricate gilded frame is a column which can be moved aside to reveal a secret compartment with the most scintillating painting of two lovers, naked and entwined. A smile eases across Simonetta's lips.

Art and ardor are combined. Only in Florence could such a delightful and imaginative design be created. And here I am years later still asking myself who those two lovers might be. Are they Lorenzo de' Medici and his mistress, Lucrezia Donati, who have caused so much gossip? Or could they be Piero and the woman rumored to be his mistress whose name no one will reveal? I certainly hope not. How insufferable. Perhaps the man is Alfonso, my ardent suitor, the handsome Duke of Calabria, soon to be King of Naples, cavorting with one of his many conquests. How lovely to guess. But of course I always end up wishing that Giuli and I are those two lovers. I can never even look at this mirror without fantasizing I am with him. Giuli…

Oh, Giuli, my love. I can just imagine how Botticelli would paint us. The two of us are lying on the grass unclothed just as the couple in the painting. No, no, my love, we are not completely unclothed, but temptingly bare. You have your camicia draped discreetly over… dare I say which part of your anatomy? Your head is thrown back and there is a smile on your face. What are you envisioning, my love?

I, so very happy, am covered in a subtly revealing, thoroughly exquisite white Alexandrian silk, strewn with gardenias. Heavenly gardenias. The soft silk of my gown drapes over my body, its touch the lightest prick of Cupid's arrow. I am transported. I want to run my fingers through your curly hair. I long to feel the strength of your arms responding to my cupped hands as I move them from your shoulder to the tips of your fingers. But, no, I must not go on, my love. I am blushing. Every cell of my body is alert. I am Venus; you are Mars.

Simonetta laughs out loud at her musings, then quickly makes the sign of the Cross, forcing her mind from her playful wanderings. She wonders that she can stand on the top step still awaiting Consolata's knock and yet inhabit such a world of delicious desire. She has become more and more adept at leaving her present life in this room and escaping into another world, erotic or not. Often without noticing, she finds herself drifting into memories of her early days in Florence.

From the moment my bridal procession rode into this town, I have loved this city. Brunelleschi's dome seemed afire from the setting sun which threw a warm glow over the entire city. I was intrigued and mystified then. I still am.

What magic is there here whose secrets I can not know? I have asked myself this question over and over. I have wanted to understand everything about this city, to become acquainted with each of its inhabitants. To visit every garden, every building, every workshop, every studio. Although I have spent days trying to explore the smallest street, each modest church, every illusive secret, there are still many mysteries that elude me.

Turning back to the window, Simonetta opens the glass panels and leans out over the chilly stone sill.

There it is. The Arno flowing swiftly with the spring thaw. Its furor fills me with a sense of abandon I have rarely felt during these last weeks. Today, I will no longer be Piero Vespucci's daughter-in-law to be bartered to procure favors. I will again be my mother's youngest and most beloved child. I will imagine I am free. I will take flight over Florence, soaring as a hawk would soar. Perhaps one of Lorenzo's hawks. High over Florence. High over the hills.

Abruptly, Simonetta takes her elbows from the window sill and stands upright.

What a dreamer I am! I cannot seem to stop myself from trying to be the poet I wish to be. If only I could capture what I see as Dante or Poliziano do. Perhaps someday I will write poems as

worthy of admiration as theirs. But for now, I will continue trying
to express the beauty I see in my own simple words.

> The hills above Santo Spirito
> are bathed in morning silk.
> The rooftops on the other side of the river
> offer their terra cotta tiles to the sun.
> Here and there, for a second or so,
> near San Frediano,
> a glint from some window appears.
> Just beyond the falling Arno
> in the shallow pool created by the little dam,
> fishermen ply their nets.
> They never fail to fill their baskets
> With trout and eel.

With a smile at her ineptitude, Simonetta settles
her elbows on the window ledge again and continues
nonetheless.

> As I listen to the rhythmic movements
> of the nets slapping the water
> below the Santa Rosa weir,
> I remember the comforting sound
> of my father's knees slapping
> against the sides of our horse
> as I ride behind him
> through the meadows of the plateau

high above our home.
I think of the many nights
I have stood at my window
searching the distance
to see Portovenere
laying calm against the sea.
I think of our very own stars
sparkling in the clear cobalt sky
undisturbed by any earthly light.
I think of home.

2

Home. I can smell the sea air as if I were standing at the top of the hill behind our farmhouse looking down over the tiny sheltered marina of our own village of Fezzano. Here in the early morning, the fishermen tend to their boats and mend their nets before setting out along the coastline of the Gulf of La Spezia, which snakes in and out as far as Portovenere where it juts out into the sea. There on the promontory the temple of Venus once stood protecting our ships as they set out to sea and welcoming merchant ships coming to our shores from other parts of the world. San Pietro, our small parish church, now stands on that same jagged point, its simple silhouette outlined against the Ligurian sky.

Liguria. Just the name brings back memories of rugged terrain and fierce harbors, but also of tranquil austere beauty. I remember the day when Gaspi took me by horseback from home across the stony hilltops to Riomaggiore, the first of the towns along the Cinque Terre. There I saw the sea water smash against the rocks of the harbor and rise to the height of twenty men before crashing down. When the boats waiting at anchor were finally hauled in, the waves were so violent the sailors could not move from boat to land without the help of ropes. What a contrast to our own marinas which sit safe inside our little bay.

There, above Fezzano, our Cattaneo family compound occupies almost the whole of the hillside. Outside the back gate of our large stone house are flower and herb gardens which reach almost to the top of the hill, just before the plateau. Consi and I would run up the hill to the fields where the wheat was undulating in the wind and play for hours among the stalks, chasing each other and taking turns hiding behind a live oak tree or a tall clump of grass. Past the wheat fields, in between Portovenere and Riomaggiore on the western side of the promontory, our vineyards of Vermentino grapes still run almost down to the sea.

So many memories. In late summer each year, the whole family went up to the vineyard to bring lunch to the contadini harvesting the grapes. Consi and I helped my mother carry large picnic baskets with enough food to feed our own family as well as those farmhands and their families who were also helping. Dozens of people. My older brothers set up a long table under one of the olive trees that were planted among the rows of vines. Then Consi and I covered it with a long linen cloth so my mother could set out the food.

So much food. Loaves of focaccia, pecorino cheese, prosciutto, salami of wild boar, roasted peppers, anchovies, seasoned olives, olive oil in abundance and fresh fruit. Large carafes of chilled water and demijohns of last year's wine were scattered among the platters.

While the rest of the family prepared for the throng of

31

hungry people, I sometimes sat with my back against a tree and let my eyes trace the procession of vines up the slope in front of me until they disappeared over the top of the hill. I watched the workers stripping the vines of their clusters which they tossed into the large willow baskets scattered along the rows. Many of the baskets were already spilling over with luscious looking light green grapes. Soon everyone stopped their work and gathered around the table to eat and tease my mother about the bounty of her lunches.

For the next few days after the harvest, my mother supervised the culling and pressing of the grapes. Consi and I sat for the whole day listening to the jokes and enjoying the singing of the workers. We watched as each basket of grapes was emptied and crushed in the huge wooden press. It seemed forever before a barrel was filled with juice, loaded on the dray behind the horses and pulled across the hill to the dusky shed which hid the entrance to the cellar dug deep into the ground on the north side of the house.

Consi and I helped too. Every time a wheel barrel was filled with discarded grape hulls, the two of us scrambled to our feet, and one at each handle, pushed the wheelbarrow across the road to the waiting cart. One of the field hands added the acrid smelling skins to those already in the cart so he could haul them to his family's farmhouse where they were pressed again to make the wine for the workers. Next the two of us pulled the empty wheelbarrow back across the packed dirt and waited to repeat the process. As a reward for our work, we were allowed all the grape juice we could drink. Its taste was so succulent that to this day I prefer my mother's grape juice to the most costly wine.

My mother supervised the servants in everything they

prepared for our family. When they ground the wheat with stones or pulverized the chestnuts to make flour for bread and pasta, she made sure no little stones or shells were ground in. When they pressed the olives to make the fresh oil, she watched that they used only the best olives. She took care that the cheese was wrapped properly, the garlic woven into even braids, the fruit and vegetables thoroughly dried before they were taken to the cellar. The salted meat was hung in the smoke house according to the traditions of her family.

In the early fall, just as the elms began to turn, my mother made huge bowls of pesto which were stored in glazed earthenware jugs for use the rest of the year. She did not permit the servants to help, not even to strip and wash the basil leaves. She was sole proprietress of her pesto. All winter she added spoonfuls of it to sauces and soups or ladled cupfuls over the fresh pasta the servants made. Since that time I have eaten many expensive, even imported, delicacies, but to this day, the meals made with my mother's pesto please me the most.

Although I was only four, I was the one appointed to gather the sweet smelling basil that proliferated around the brick wall of our garden. When I was ready to return with Consi from the gathering, the square flat baskets were so large and piled so high we needed to call for help to carry them into the house.

Gaspi always came running from the loggia where he was having his coffee or doing his accounting. He gathered up first, not the basket, but me in his arms, swinging me round and round, basil flying everywhere as he proclaimed in a loud voice.

"My daughter is the Princess of Basil."

33

And then he pretended to be sniffing my neck before setting me down.

"Hmmm. She smells so good, I cannot tell which plant is the real one."

The smell of summer. The smell of the plains. The smell of crushed pine nuts, chopped garlic, and new olive oil combined with basil in perfect proportion. Inhale. Take in the whole of it. The steaming pasta beneath, the grated pecorino romano on top, and my mother's laughter.

My mother. Caterina Violante Spinola Campofregoso Cattaneo. Just the name evokes the sound of her clear, ringing voice. Everyone calls her by her familiar name, Catocchia. Even I. Catocchia. Mother of 14 children. Old enough in years to be my grandmother. Young enough in manner and looks to be my sister. How I adore her!

Sometimes when Consi and I were in the kitchen alone with her, she would tell us of her life with her first husband, Il Doge for One Day, Battista Campofregoso. I laughed every time she told about how he had tried to usurp the place of the true Doge, his brother, while his brother was in the countryside one day combating a rebellion. The rebellion had been suppressed and Battista's attempted coup had failed, but his brother had not punished him. By forgiving him, his brother had made Battista an ally for the rest of his life.

A forlorn look would pass over Catocchia's face and with much gravity, she would repeat how Battista, the father of Battistina and Pietro whom I had come to love as I did my other brothers and sisters, was killed five years later trying to defend that same brother.

But Catocchia is never sad for long. She has known great sorrow, but she has also known great happiness. She has enjoyed much wealth and prestige in Genoa because of her noble Spinola family and also because of my half brother Pietro who became Doge of Genoa. Still Catocchia relishes the simple life she has found in this part of Liguria with Gaspi. He has given her many reasons for joy. Much laughter. Twelve more children. And love enough to last a hundred lifetimes.

Oh, dearest Mother, I think of you so often. Of how we are alike in many ways. We have each inhabited two different worlds, but we are each more content in a world of simplicity and natural beauty than in a world of wealth and noble position. We both take delight in the beauty of the world around us and give thanks to God for his blessings. But most of all, we both love with abandon. Long ago you taught me that a woman's capacity for love is her greatest endowment. The more expansive her love, the greater her happiness. And sometimes, sadly, the more intense her sorrow.

Dearest Catocchia, my dear mother, you have taught me more than I will ever realize, much through your stories but most through your life. Right now I have only one wish. I long to be held in your arms again. To sense the warmth of your body. To smell on your skin the aromas of your cooking. To feel safe.

Simonetta turns from the window and makes her way down the two stone steps toward the writing table by the door. Centered on the table is a small gilded chest with a delicate ceramic image of the Madonna on the lid. It was her husband Marco's wedding gift to her. In this chest, as her mother taught her, Simonetta keeps the copies she has made of important letters she has written. Here, too, are copies of her letters to her mother, including the ones she most values with her first impressions of her new life. The excitement. The novelty. Even the reluctant acknowledgment of her doubts.

Simonetta opens the cassetta and takes out the first of these letters. She unfolds its worn pages cautiously and begins to read.

Dearest and Most Revered Mother,

I do not understand what compulsion pulls me quite early from my bed on a morning so soon after the last of my marriage feasts. Perhaps it is the excitement I feel at knowing when I throw open the shutters, I will see the splendor of the Arno snaking its way toward the west like a glittering necklace embellishing this rare city I have already begun to love. Perhaps it is my anticipation of the coming days.

Happily, I am at least somewhat settled here in Florence. The delightful easy days of celebrating my betrothal with our whole family in Piombino seem long ago. Even the wedding trip, which was arduous but exhilarating, already seems far in the past. Unfortunately, only the stop at Pisa provided the accommodations and comforts I had hoped to have on the entire journey. But I do not mean to complain. Despite many discomforts, we encountered extraordinary beauty along the way and the people we met were both hospitable and jolly.

My welcome to Marco's home on Via Ognissanti was splendid. The Vespucci family treated me as an honored guest. All three of our wedding feasts were more sumptuous than any I have ever known. Marco says his family may even be censured by the Medici for its lavishness. Evidently Cosimo the Elder had admonished his Medici sons and grandsons that extravagance is not comely. He counseled them that "plenty for all" should be the goal of a truly great man. But you know my father-in-law, Piero. He is not worried. In truth, he holds that these feasts are a way to increase his importance with the Medici.

Marco declared that the generous wedding gifts sent from the Medici are a mark of their esteem and indicate the Vespucci family's rise in the world. Then he looked at me with that sly little grin of his and said in all probability the splendor of the gifts is a reflection of the growing renown of my beauty. The Medici brothers are reputed to be aficionados of great beauty in all its forms. My Marco excels in teasing me about "my beauty" even though I refuse to take him seriously. As you have taught me, I, too, believe a woman's desirability is not enhanced by vanity, but enriched by the virtues she harbors inside.

Had you told me when I was younger that I would be living in an environment so lavish and vibrant, I would have thought you were trying to amuse me. That you were imagining me as a fairy princess or even Venus herself. But I must confess that having my handsome Marco at my side, being dressed like a queen, watching the delights of my wedding feasts unfold, each one more elaborate than the previous, have all captured my imagination as well.

Dearest Mother, although only a few weeks have passed, I regret your absence already. How I wish you and Father had been able to accompany me to Florence and stay a while with me here. The days you and I had together at Piombino before my wedding were precious, but too few and too long ago. I am sorely in need of your presence and your counsel as I try to negotiate my way into this new life. Only my excitement at so much to learn and so much beauty to appreciate can drag my thoughts from the days of tranquil pleasures as your beloved daughter.

Please, dearest Mother, rest assured I am well and have every comfort. Even though from time to time I may stumble as I adjust to the great changes in my situation, I am not unhappy. I am captivated and intrigued. I only hope I will soon have the great fortune of sharing my many experiences with you in person.

Tell Gaspi I am well and happy except for missing the two of you and the joy I have always felt in our dear family home.

I await your first letter with impatience, my dearest Mother. How much I miss you.

Please accept my greatest respect, my strong and undying love. I embrace you both.

Simonetta allows the letter to drop from her hand onto the writing table. She stares at the wall in front of her. She traces its design around the circumference of the room. There is a slight crease on her brow and the hint of a smile on her lips, as if she is both puzzled and pleased at the same time.

Why must I always be reminded of Piero when I am in this room? Although I do not ask it, do not want it, he insists on trying to please me. Even when I look at these walls, I am forced to remember that Piero is the one who employed apprentices from the most prestigious workshops in Florence to paint them with my favorite color, rich pomegranate. And what disbursals he made for the pigments, especially the Chinese vermilion! I should be grateful to him and I do have to admit, albeit reluctantly, the entire effect is beautiful. The walls look as if they are covered with finely embossed velvet.

How patient the artists were with my unending questions. One of them explained the layering process that they must apply over the plaster. A series of glazes, each one producing a richer color because of the one before. Oranges, burnt umbers, ochres, vermilions, each mixed with egg yolk and oil. Tempera grassa, they called it. The result is a brilliance whose depth invites me to dive into its colors.

In everything, I see color first. That is why I have always wanted to become a painter. But the artists here study for years and work a lifetime to achieve their art. I could never have the patience to produce such subtle and intricate designs. I cannot imagine dedicating a lifetime to learning how to paint. The smell alone would discourage me.

Of course, there is something else which inhibits me from pursuing my interest in painting. Something more important which makes me angry to think on. Women are prohibited from using oils. I have heard this restriction is because the ores used to produce the pigments are very dangerous for an unborn child. However, I am sure that is not the only reason for the restriction. Women are also prohibited from engaging in many other endeavors. We cannot attend the University. We are not permitted to participate in public governance. The only property a woman is permitted to own is her dowry, which remains in the control of her husband until his death.

I have been fortunate to live among those who believe themselves to be Humanists and who accept that women are equal to men in intellect and creativity. These men not only believe in the innate worth of women, but they also encourage and assist the women who share their lives in developing and using the abilities each has been given. How grateful I am to have been born into this time of changing attitudes.

Sadly, I have no aptitude for drawing and I have never learned how to mix pigments. I will never be able to produce the vibrant colors I see in my mind. Still I would like to be able to capture the color of the summer sky as it appears behind the fortification on the cliffs across the bay from Portovenere. The deep navy of the water in between. To reproduce the color of red pears in late summer, hanging against the turning leaves. To replicate the pale yellow of the fields after the wheat has been cut in fall. Or imitate the brilliant palette of my darling little Botticelli whose paintings and frescoes are the best in Florence.

I suppose I must accept that I will need to capture any beauty I perceive with my words.

Simonetta picks up the letter from her writing table and carefully refolds it.

4

Simonetta opens the cassetta, replaces the first letter on top of the others and pulls a second from beneath it. She opens it quickly. She is moving like someone hungry for more food, impatient to reread those experiences which have caused so many changes within her.

Most Revered Mother,

How different life in the Vespucci household is from my life in Fezzano and Piombino with you and our loud fun-loving family. The house here on Via Ognissanti is cold and dark. Despite all the politeness I am shown and all the comforts I am given, there is an iciness which pervades the air. And so much silence. There are no sounds of children or laughter, not even of arguments. There are no servants bustling around. The servants are kind and helpful, but they move quietly from place to place as if afraid of being reprimanded. They keep their heads down and curtsy when they pass.

Consi says she can leave my room and walk as far as the garden without seeing anyone, not even a servant, or hearing any chatter or sounds of movement. She is hoping to make friends with at least a few of the other servants, but for now, she takes solace in listening to the chanting of the Umiliata at their offices in the cloister next door.

Marco's family members barely speak to one another and Piero seldom talks to anyone except me, demanding my attentions and prating about his accomplishments. Piero's mother, whom we call Nonna, is still mourning the long ago death of her husband. She wears a black habit always and much like the Carmelite nuns who have taken the vow of silence, she has retreated into a life of prayer and meditation. She is a phantom-like figure around the house. Although she has been given the responsibility of seeing to my religious education, she takes little interest in me and prefers instead to pray most of the day. Even when we are all together at dinner, she keeps her head bowed and addresses no one.

Marco's sisters also sit very quietly. One of his sisters will marry, but the other two have been promised to the Church. Since Marco is the only male child, the Vespucci must trust in me to provide them with an heir. Already I sense Piero looking at me skeptically, wondering if I will be able to give Marco a child. Consi tells me that in some families here, the marriage is consummated and the bride is pregnant even before the wedding festivities begin.

Marco's dear mother, Caterina, sees to the running of the house and is as quiet as the servants she supervises. But she is a loving woman and already she has brought me several small gifts from her treasures. She also presents me with tasty treats from her kitchen nearly every day. Even though she seems to be burdened with a melancholy from which she rarely escapes, she has a softness about her which helps me feel more and more comfortable here.

Marco, however, is another matter. For me, he is an enigma. He

43

is a timid boy for all his fifteen years and usually happy despite his father. We are like children together. But our marriage is not at all what I had thought marriage would be.

Dear Mother, you are my confidante and friend. Perhaps you can help me understand. I am in need of your counsel. When Marco and I sleep together, he will often say goodnight and turn his body away from me although I might wish for more. When he touches me, he is without enthusiasm, and he seems only to be performing a prescribed duty. I respond to him in the same way, as he gives me no reason to do otherwise.

Please, dear Mother, do not despair. Our intimacy is without joy, but our friendship is warm and consoling. I am sure we will soon begin to have a union of both our hearts and our bodies.

Piero treats Marco like a little boy who does not know the rules of the game he is playing. Marco goes everywhere with him, following behind and engaging in discussions or pleasantries with the other youth whom they might meet. Piero pays attention only to the details of his own position and seems indifferent to what poor Marco may say or think. Although Piero has long been respected as a representative of the Medici court, when he talks of his duties, he seems wary of everything he says. Since the attempt on Piero de' Medici's life several years ago, rumors of rebellion in the Republic abound, and everyone is suspicious of everyone else. Each knows any one of them could be guilty of traitorous thoughts or actions.

In these first few weeks, Piero has called me several times to his study on the first floor, the studiolo of which he is so proud. There he points out some statue of great value he has had commissioned or a costly object he has acquired in his mercantile travels. I try not to imagine myself as one of those objects that he spares no expense in procuring and protecting until the time is ripe for it to bring him the best possible price. However, I do *have the impression I am being carefully groomed for some role which will enhance his standing in the Medici court.*

Piero has had me fitted for the most luxurious clothes in the latest fashions. He has commissioned the hairdresser to weave my hair with ornaments of gold and pearls which he provides. Yesterday he presented me with an extraordinary length of black pearls from his travels to the South Seas...

Simonetta blanches at what her mother does not know. What she has not written into this letter.

As clearly as if it were only yesterday, she remembers how Piero looked at her as he pulled those pearls from the black velvet pouch that held them. He smiled at her in a way that made her feel as if she had done something wrong. Then he walked slowly around his writing table, never taking his eyes off her, and stood so close to her arm that if she had moved, she would have touched his breeches.

Next Piero pulled back her hair which had not yet been dressed and ran his finger lightly along the nape of her neck. She sat frozen. She was afraid to move. Afraid to say a word.

"You are such a beautiful girl, Simonetta," he whispered, bending his head close to her ear. With his arms reaching around her shoulders, he placed the pearls on the front of her morning coat, then pulled them around her neck. Gently parting her hair in the back, he hooked the clasp. His breath was warm on her neck and she felt goose bumps gathering under her skin.

Simonetta knew that her next words would decide the course of her young life. She moved slightly away from Piero, looked up at him and said, "Signore, you are such a generous father-in-law. I know Marco will be pleased to see me in these pearls. He admires your taste in everything. And the Medici will be most impressed to know that you are magnanimous in your gifts to both your son and his wife."

Piero turned and walked back around to his side of the writing desk.

"You may go now, Simonetta."

"Thank you, sir, for your gift."

Simonetta took a deep breath. That day she had passed her first test. But she had been sure this would not be the last time she would have to use her cunning to escape what she did not want to endure.

Quickly, Simonetta looks back at the letter, hoping to be distracted from the shame she is feeling. Even though she is aware of the burning sensation on her cheeks, she continues reading.

. . . In addition, Piero has engaged a tutor to give me instruction on the history and manners of the Florentine nobility. I do not know how I will manage to fulfill his expectations. Nor do I wish to. Were it not for Marco's attentions to me and our private talks together, I think I should be totally swallowed up by Piero's aspirations.

Do not dismay, dear Mother. I would be the first to admit that having any part in Piero's manipulations is more interesting than sitting in a dusky room with the other women of this household. They seem all too satisfied to limit their artistic endeavors to needlework, I need much more to make me content. Listening to the forced conversations between these kind but boring women is one of the few burdens I am forced to bear. I can tolerate my fingers being idle from time to time, but I cannot abide an idle mind. To be forced to focus on mundane considerations is tantamount to torture for me.

Although I do sit quietly with the women each morning, I am sketching or writing in my journal, which is one of the ways I escape this daily trial. I am experimenting with poetry as I learned that everyone here writes it. Although I have given you little reason to know how important my writing still is to me, you may recall how I used to sit for hours on a great rock just in sight of our house while Consi did her chores. Even then, I was challenging myself to see and hear farther and farther. I was trying to imagine the worlds beyond Portovenere and pretend that well-appointed ships would carry me away to exotic lands of abundance. To places where feasts of sensuality would be waiting for me. Feasts for the eyes, for the body, for the soul.

How I do digress. But I am very serious about my writing. So far, my poetry seems immature and unsophisticated, but I am sure my skill will grow as I continue to practice. There are so many accomplished poets in Florence. Lorenzo de' Medici's mother, Lucrezia, is a fine poet and her works, although mainly religious, are quite respected. She reads them at gatherings among the intellectuals, the nobles and the foreign dignitaries. She has also published a book of instruction on how to run a household which is more frequently consulted than any other book in Florence. She is a central personage in the Platonic Society. And just as you insisted for me, she has made sure that Lorenzo and Giuliano have had the finest education in classical studies. They too can read and write Latin and Greek.

Lorenzo de' Medici is also a poet. Piero says he keeps a poetry journal, in addition to a log of historical events and a personal journal, all of which he writes in every day. It would seem to me that he would have little time for governance with all the writing he does. Even Giuliano, his brother, writes poetry, although Consolata tells me that he enjoys playing at games or dancing more than pursuing his writings or any of his studies.

It will not be long until I learn more about these Medici brothers who seem to be the center of all life here, cultural, social, artistic and political. In only a few more days, the Vespucci family will be attending Lorenzo's grand tournament. The whole city has been preparing for months. Lorenzo de' Medici has the reputation of giving the most magnificent of entertainments to which everyone in the city is invited. He is known to be versed in every skill, especially in the chivalric and amorous ones.

The young Giuliano de' Medici is reputed to be the most handsome, well endowed, and charming of all the young men of Florence. Consi says he will ride in his brother's tournament although he is just as young as I. I cannot wait to see him for the first time for myself. How eager I am for that day to come.

Rest assured, dear Mother, I am trying to profit from the many experiences I have encountered here. Piero introduces me to intriguing personages who speak many languages and discuss the most challenging ideas. He takes me about town to see extraordinary artistic and architectural accomplishments.

Each day during devotionals, I pray that God will grant me the ability to embrace the grace and wonder of His world. I pray that I will become an embodiment of His beauty. That He will bless me with a lifetime of learning. Especially of learning how to see.

I am still awaiting your first letter. I am hungry for news of home. Although my life is exciting and full, I will forever miss the joys of my life with you and Gaspi.

I remain, as always, your youngest devotee.
May God watch over you and my beloved Gaspi,

Your most loving, Simonetta
Via Borgo Ognissanti
Florence
4 February 1469

5

Trying not to make the least noise, Consolata turns the handle of the door very slowly. Surely, someone will soon notice that the locksmith needs to be called to repair the rusty old iron piece. As she looks into the room, she sees Simonetta in bed.

As usual, the tray Consolata carries is beautifully arranged with fine linen napkins taken from among those Catocchia embroidered years ago for her daughter's trousseau. With the exception of the cream-colored egg cup which Simonetta brought from home, Consolata uses the porcelain with the Vespucci family crest that Piero purchased in China when he was still a merchant-captain. She judges this china a bit ornate for a breakfast tray, but she does as she is told.

Each morning Consolata sends one of the servants to the garden for a fresh flower or a bit of greenery to place in the small ceramic vase Caterina gave Simonetta when they first arrived. Then, Consolata, who loves color as well as her mistress, adds the vase to the veritable tableau of bowls and plates brimming with fresh fruits and jams.

When they first arrived, Simonetta had given Consi a wooden box of colored chalks and a folio, hoping they might help to divert her from her loneliness. These are Consolata's most prized possessions. Whenever she can steal away from her chores, she spends her free time in the Vespucci gardens sketching the fruits and flowers. Sometimes she even peeps over the wall to sketch the trees and arches of the Umiliata cloisters next door. Her drawings are wild with color and uninhibited by convention. Simonetta loves them. She avers they are a perfect reflection of her friend's flamboyant personality. Consi simply laughs at this assertion.

After she sets the tray down, Consolata tiptoes over to the bed and waits for Simonetta to stir. She is not sure what to do next.

Simonetta takes very little to eat these days. She has not been feeling well for weeks, even before Lorenzo and Giuliano left for Pisa. Her mother-in-law has hinted that she might at last be pregnant, but Simonetta is only saddened by the thought. She believes she has no hope of carrying a child full term. However she can not help wondering about what is happening in her body right now. She feels sure there is no pregnancy. Recently, there has been word that the Plague is spreading in northern Italy, although no hint of it has arrived in any of the towns or villages nearby.

As soon as Simonetta gives a little stir, Consolata says softly, "Good morning, my lady. Did you sleep well?"

"As well as can be expected, Consolata. But I will confess, these nights I do not sleep so very well at all."

"I have good news this morning, my lady. Signor Vespucci received a letter from il Magnifico yesterday announcing that he is sending round his own doctor, Maestro Stefano, late this afternoon. Signor Vespucci seems most pleased that il Magnifico considers you his esteemed friend and he is impressed by il Magnifico's concern for you."

"Ah, yes, Consi, as you know, my father-in-law is always happy to receive attention from the Medici. Please believe me, dear Consi, I do not feel so very ill that Lorenzo should trouble himself to send his own doctor. A little cough. A little loss of appetite. And I am sure this tiny loss of weight will certainly serve me well when I am putting on my new dress for Giuliano's return.

"Do the servants have any gossip, Consi? I would love to hear what is being said around town about this recent trip to Pisa these Medici friends of mine have undertaken. And without any compelling reason that I can ascertain. They profess some excuse having to do with the university, but I am doubtful that can be the sole reason for spending so much time in Pisa in this season when the hunting is excellent there."

Simonetta smiles at her own facetiousness, then continues.

"Do you remember when Giuliano was sent to the university by Lorenzo to appease the citizens after the massacre at Volterra? All we heard was that his main studies at the university were dancing, jousting, and hunting. So then, what are we to think of this current journey? From what Giuliano writes in his only letter thus far, I can discern not a particle of what is really happening."

"My lady, the news is somewhat old, but the gossip is that Signor Poliziano wrote Madonna Clarice from San Miniato on the way to Pisa several weeks ago. It sounds very much as if il Magnifico is his same vibrant self. Signor Poliziano reported he tried to observe Lent by reading to the men from Saint Augustine, but ended up observing it instead by drinking good wine, being brilliant and keeping the company entertained with his bawdy lyrics and dancing. And Signor Giuliano with him."

Consolata puts her hand over her mouth to conceal the silly grin that appears there.

Simonetta lets a little laugh escape and pushes herself up against the backboard of the bed before speaking.

"Madonna Clarice is always concerned when her husband is away. She seems to take solace in pretending Lorenzo's love of hawking is his sole obsession and the one which occupies his time when he is not overseeing the renovation of the buildings at the university."

Simonetta continues, "Is there no other word of Giuliano?"

"I have heard none, my lady."

"I must write him as soon as I have eaten. Please, Consi, bring the folio of papers from the antechamber and fill my inkwell again. I have decided to begin writing right away, before even dressing. As for breakfast this morning, I don't think I will take anything more than a bit of warm milk with sugar, which you can place on the writing table."

Suddenly, as if even the thought of getting out of bed is too tiring, Simonetta lies back on the pillows.

Just as Consolata turns toward the door, Simonetta lets out a sigh.

"Thank you, dear Consi. What would I do without you here? You are the bit of radiance that comes into this room each day to remind me of how beautiful life can be. I have been too preoccupied with my own concerns. What of you?"

Consolata nears the bed again.

Simonetta has a sly grin as she continues.

"Are you still listening to that very special voice from beyond our walls? A lovely voice, no, that of Father Giovanni, the new parish priest next door? There is a rumor you pause often in your work to hear his melodic chants. It has also been reported that there appears a dreamy look in your eyes as you listen. I would not be surprised to find a small peep hole carved into the wall of the back garden that gives onto the cloister."

Consi smiles. She is accustomed to such teasing from her mistress.

Simonetta continues. "The servants have told me the Father is red-headed and quite a handsome young man, especially for one of the Order of the Umiliata. They say he is much abashed when he comes near you in the street. They giggle and try to guess what miracle may be hidden under those coarse brown robes."

Now Simonetta is the one who is smiling as she delivers these words.

"Is it true you are going to Mass more often than ever? I can imagine this new young priest has quite a warm touch with those praying hands. Am I wrong, Consi? "

Trying to regain control over her reddening face and lowered eyes, Consolata raises her head and answers quickly.

"I wouldn't know about these things, Madonna. I simply do my work," she answers in mock seriousness. "But I will confess I have attended Mass more often recently. To pray for your rapid recovery, of course."

"As always, Consi, I believe you. But that sparkle in your eyes reveals a lot more than your words."

As Consolata exits the room, Simonetta's thoughts are still focused on her dear friend and companion.

Poor Consi. She is not very happy here, but she tries to make me happy. Her presence in any room already makes it seem warmer and more like home. Even now at twenty-five, she is still a vibrant hardy woman, rosy of complexion and of such good spirits. She would make a fine wife for someone.

She should have a husband and children of her own.

And I, I have almost given up hope holding a sweet baby of my own in my arms. Of singing sweet lullabies. Of teaching my child to love the flowers and the trees and the sun as I do. How I long so to bring a child into this world. If I ever have a child, I will arrange a marriage for Consolata, too, so Consi can become the wet nurse for all my babies.

Just the thought of the two of them together with their own children brings tears to Simonetta's eyes.

Consi reminds me I am still young and when the time comes, I will be able to produce a child. I do so want to believe her, but I am not convinced. I... But enough. I must not allow myself to think on it.

Simonetta has already decided that if Piero is not disposed to help Consolata find a husband, she will appeal to Lorenzo for money from the fund Lucrezia has established to provide dowries for the poorer girls of Florence. Lucrezia is determined to help these young women who otherwise would be condemned to become the lowest of servants in someone else's home or in a convent serving the nuns. Lucrezia has also used the funds to help other women who do not have a dowry sufficient to make a good match. These women would have been forced to pay such money as they had to become nuns in order to have a secure life. Like Lucrezia, Simonetta is appalled that over half of all women in Florence end up without a home of their own. She cannot help but wonder what would have happened to Consi if she had remained with her birth family.

Simonetta slides down into the covers, stretches her body out to its full length, and closes her eyes. Her thoughts turn to Giuliano.

6

Holding perfectly still under the covers with her eyes still closed, Simonetta begins composing the letter to Giuliano she will write down word for word later.

My dear and most beloved Giuli,

Please receive my sincere respects. I trust you and Lorenzo are well and enjoying the pleasures of Pisa. I think of that city as a priceless little jewel, shining white even when the sun is not, and so much closer to the delights of the sea than we. I hope for your sake the weather is warm there. Here, unfortunately for us, an April chill still holds.

Just this morning I have learned of the correspondence between Lorenzo and Piero about my illness. Lorenzo is always so attentive and solicitous that he is like a brother. Although I am most grateful for his diligence and especially for his caring, I do believe he makes too much fuss over me. I hope it will please the both of you not to worry yourselves for my health while you are away.

Contrary to Piero's evaluation, I seem to be doing better than when you left. I am, as you must have noted, often at my table writing to you and also to Mother. I am taking more food now and stand frequently at my window anticipating your return. I have become quite adroit at envisioning you coming along the road from Pisa, through the Porto al Prato, and down Via Borgo Ognissanti straight into the courtyard of our palazzo. I know your return is many weeks away, but for me, these days since you have gone already seem like centuries. As I watched you disappear beyond the gates, I felt as if I had seen you for the last time.

Please do not be distressed that I write such personal thoughts while you feel constrained not to do so for fear that Piero might intercept your letters. I have no such fear. I have gone to great lengths to assure that none of my letters to you will fall into Piero's hands. Although hearing of your activities is intriguing for me, I need few details. Just knowing that you are safe and in the same town as Lorenzo is a comfort. I will admit, however, your presence is a solace I sorely lack these days.

My dear Giuliano, there are no words to tell you what sustenance you and Lorenzo have brought me over the years. What joy you have added to my life. How much I have learned from both of you and how much I love you both. I cannot bear to think of what my life in Florence would have been without sharing it with each of you.

Lorenzo has been my light, the protector of my spirit and thoughts, my shining knight, the example of wisdom and fairness. But you, Giuliano, have been all that and much more. You are my one great love. This truth I want you to know so that whatever happens, we can each take this knowledge with us to our graves.

Sadly, you are not with me now and given my effusiveness in this letter, you must think me the silly little girl of fifteen that you saw the day we met for the first time at Lorenzo's tournament. Please remember me as I am now and think of the richness of our present love. I will take heart, for it will be only a little longer until I can enjoy that richness again. I am sure I will have my full strength by the time you return. Simply by writing you, I already feel so much stronger that I am certain I could run down the stairs with the lightest of steps and dash out to meet you in the full sun.

I close with much regret that I cannot continue to write forever, and with a heavy heart that we are not together. Though I await our reunion with impatience, I send you many good wishes for your excursions of hawking and hunting in the days to come.

Give my continuing respects to Lorenzo.

I pray that you will hold me in your heart, now and forever, as I hold you.

God be eternally with you.
Your most ardent admirer and devoted friend,
Simonetta Vespucci
Florence, 18 April 1476

Part II

20 April 1476

Your most honorable imminence and esteemed friend, Lorenzo, Il Magnifico,

A little while ago I wrote to you and told you of the illness of Simonetta and now for the Grace of God and by the virtue of Maestro Stefano, by your intercession, she is rather better. She has less fever and vomiting, and less shortness of breath from the lungs, eats better and sleeps better, but from what the doctor says, her sickness will be long and little remedy can be done, if she is not carefully cared for. If she gets out of this state because of this goodness of yours, all of us and her mother who is at Piombino, all thank you, and are humbled by the attention you have shown about this illness of hers. I am afraid, however, of being indiscreet and over presumptuous in showing my gratitude toward the honorable Maestro. (In this matter, I will trust in your advice and help. Our gratitude is endless, but our means are limited.) Thus, we would never be able to compensate with any amount of payment for this extraordinary service should we offer all that we have to give…

Your most humble servant, Piero Vespucci
Florence, Italy, 20 April 1476

7

"No! No!

Lorenzo! Lorenzo!

I am coming! I am coming to help you."

My voice is so loud and so full of fright I am sure it can be heard outside Il Duomo as far away as the Medici palace. Through the shadows I see the knife descend. Once. Twice. A third time. But I hear nothing. In the dim light, I can barely make out the distant face of Lorenzo. I thrust out both arms, trying to reach him, but Lorenzo's face keeps fading from me as I move toward him. I will not leave Lorenzo in danger nor will I leave the Cathedral while danger is anywhere near him.

Then he is gone. The dagger is gone. What remains surprises me. In the crowd close to where Lorenzo had stood, I catch a glimpse of my father-in-law, Piero.

But where is Giuliano? Where is my love?

Simonetta lies for a long time without opening her eyes. As she lies there, she thinks of the recent rumors of renewed threats against Lorenzo and Giuliano by the Pazzi family. Giuliano had told her that even before she arrived in Florence, the Pazzi had made an attempt on his father's life. Later she had overheard the women at Lorenzo's wedding whisper about a plan to assassinate both the father and the two brothers. Since Piero de' Medici's early death from gout in that same year, there had been even more reason to fear a plot against Lorenzo and Giuliano.

Even as early as the time of Cosimo de' Medici, Lorenzo's grandfather, the Pazzi have been unhappy that they were second in power to the Medici. They continue to take offense at what they perceive to be the Medici's condescending treatment of them. Several years ago, Jacopo Pazzi contrived to place on the throne in Rome a pope who was favorable to his family. Just two years ago, he sent his sons to Rome to bribe that pope, Sixtus, to switch his allegiances. These young men convinced the Pope to use the Pazzi bank as the official financial establishment of the Papacy instead of continuing the Church's long-established affiliation with the Medici bank.

Once Pazzi became the bankers to Pope Sixtus, they felt entitled to be in control of the Republic of Florence. Jacopo's sons convinced the Pope that the Pazzi would be more cooperative agents than the Medici in following his dictates and protecting his vast lands and conquered territories. They even promised the Pope they would restore to the Papacy some of the lands it lost when the Medici conquered them. In addition, the elder Pazzi, Jacopo, has pledged to enlist his Florentine followers to help the Pope overthrow the Medici.

Simonetta shudders. In recent months she has heard so much about this growing threat to her friends that she cannot suppress her forebodings.

Slowly Simonetta pulls the quilts up over her shoulders again, covering her arms and refusing to open her eyes to the new day.

Lorenzo seems to think he is safe because his sister has married into the Pazzi family, but I maintain my nightmares are founded in a very present and ugly political reality. I am caught between a nightmare world where I cannot control the plot and the real world where I fight to control my destiny. Surely I can stop myself from having the same haunting dream every night, from awakening in the same cold sweat every morning.

I will think of all the lovely days of my early youth. Those days before my family was forced to flee to Piombino. I will think back to a place where danger is a word I did not yet know. If I can think of one of my favorite days from the past, I can become an innocent young girl again.

Simonetta smiles.

Without moving, I can feel my father swing me up behind him onto the horse my brother Marco brought me from Genoa as a present for my fourth birthday. We ride across the bluff at top speed, not stopping until we are almost to Doria Castle atop the hill above Portovenere. From here, we can trace the twisting road lined with olive trees that comes from the north down to the busy port and along the whole length of the quay with the several dozen houses above it.

So many times I have skipped along this seawall over the ballast stones on my way to Mass with my family at St. Peter the Apostle. I relive the scene over and over. At the end of the long wharf, I look up at the black and white striped quartz that forms a linear pattern around our church. I hurry up the many steps until I am out of breathe before I even reach the archway that leads to the tiny chapel within. Once inside the portal, I run as reverently as I can to look through the Gothic arches which are made of stone and open to permit light and air within. While the priest chants the litany in rhythm with the sound of the waves below, I am permitted to stand there with the sun on my face. I feel the ocean breeze blow through my hair as I search the distance for the three small islands that sit not far away along the coastline of Liguria.

Still feeling the warmth of the Ligurian sun, Simonetta stirs a little. The scent of basil permeates the air around her; the smell of the hillsides full of wild rosemary and thyme embrace her. Before she can manage to open her eyes and re-enter the present, she remembers how when she was barely five she was taken from all she had ever known.

Her family had been forced to flee when her half-brother, Pietro de' Campofregoso, abdicated as Doge of Genoa after the French threatened the city. Against the best interests of his countrymen, Pietro had made an elaborate agreement with the French to assure that the Campofregosi family would keep their lands and their wealth. Later, the French reneged on their promise. Then, when Pietro tried to return to Genoa to retake his land, he was stabbed to death by his own compatriots.

Simonetta's family had sought refuge with her half-sister, Battistina, and her husband, the Duke Jacopo III of the Appiani, who welcomed them into their court at Piombino. Simonetta had delighted in living among the many other children her age. She had thrived at her lessons with a tutor who devoted his time exclusively to her education. Greek, Latin, Philosophy, Art. She relished each subject. Most of all, she treasured having so many members of her family near.

Simonetta is fully awake, but her eyes are still closed.

The darkness is coming again. I cannot stop it. I cannot think of Piombino without recreating what happened there four years ago. Of the account Lorenzo's own emissary gave me of the tragedy. I cannot stop my mind from imagining I am there and reliving the whole horror.

At one of the many banquets held in the refectory where I had eaten most of my meals for the ten years I lived there, I can see the guests stand to hear Jacopo's toast. I can see my dear sister's smiling face and graceful body, always beautifully dressed. As she raises her goblet, I try to reach out and touch her. Just as I reach for her, she falls beside the banquet table, her satin dress stained with wine, blood flowing from her mouth. Jacopo's hand reaches to unsheathe his dagger just before he too falls prostrate, his body covering the platters heaped with warm food on the table before him.

Simonetta shakes uncontrollably in her bed. The sheets that were already wet with sweat are now growing cold. She continues to experience this horrific massacre as if she had been there in Piombino when it took place. A poison had been slipped into the wine, the amount precisely calculated so that just as the toast ended, all the members of the court would be overcome at their places, most with their glasses still upraised.

Dear God, thank you for sparing my brother, Stefano, and restoring him to power in Portovenere before the massacre took place. Thank you that Catocchia and Gaspi had already returned to Portovenere and were safe. I am grateful, too, dear God, that I was spared. Amen.

Still Simonetta cannot help wondering if in the future …

Most of my life, I have tottered on the edge of one nightmarish reality or another. I will forever anguish over the assassinations of Battistina, Jacopo and Pietro. I fear for those in power, those whom I love, who can never be sure when a former ally might become jealous or ambitious and try to take the power for himself. And everyone has to worry about invasions by the French or the Saracens, the Papacy or other states nearby. I must force myself to confront the raw knowledge that these times are brutal and the world is not as I wish, full of beauty and love.

Simonetta opens her eyes and tries to focus on the colors and patterns of the frescoed wall.

I should sit up in bed and welcome this new day. But the hour is early yet. The light is not strong through the shutters and I have heard no noises from below.

"My lady. My lady," she hears Consolata whisper urgently at the door, as she gives a little knock. "I have news.

And your breakfast."

"Oh, please come in, Consi," Simonetta replies as she sits up, still covered with quilts. "I have been waiting for you to wake me from my daydreaming. I miss your company. These last two days, you have been so busy and I so tired."

Consolata sets the breakfast tray on the writing table and crosses over to the bed. Before she can reveal her own news, a gush of words comes from Simonetta.

"Will you stay with me a while? I am lonely. Marco was supposed to come to me last night, but I can only guess he was cavorting around the town again with his friends. It has been weeks since he has been with me for any length of time.

"I miss laughing with him over the latest gossip about the servants and our friends. I miss being able to confide in him the little doubts that plague me from time to time. He no longer sleeps with me. On those occasions when he does visit now, he is like his father, solicitous but solemn."

"Try not to think on it, my lady. However you may be right about last night. Signor Marco is not in the house this morning. I venture to say he will return soon and go directly to bed. According to some of the other servants, Signor Vespucci is growing quite impatient with his son's nightly wanderings. But more importantly, the Signore is afraid for him.

"The gossips say there is a new mood in town

concerning the nocturnal activities of our young men. A young reformer to the north, they call him Savonarola, is preaching against all kinds of extravagant behavior. He is calling on the Church to punish what he calls the "deviant" activities like those of the brigata. Who knows what will happen if the Church listens to him. Many say Lorenzo probably will not intercede. Now that he is a serious, married man and a father as well, he no longer participates in these nightly outings. But Giuliano…"

"Please do not give me cause to be more afraid for Giuliano, Consi. I worry about him every moment. Have you heard any further word?"

"No, Madonna. No word at all of Giuliano, but there is word from il Magnifico. Signor Piero has asked me to inform you that Maestro Stefano will be paying you a visit this afternoon. It seems Lorenzo wants to assure himself that you are indeed much better and will be yourself again at their return."

"Oh, dear, Consi. Maestro Stefano's visit is yet another bother, despite the fact that he is such an affable old fellow. Of course I am grateful to Lorenzo for his concern, but I am convinced I am much improved. I simply am not inclined to receive another doctor, even Lorenzo's. However I much prefer Maestro Stefano to Maestro Moyse, Piero's dour old doctor, who continues to give me horrid medicines which make me no better. Sometimes even worse, simply from the taste of them. If I must go through this annoyance, I do hope Maestro Stefano will at least agree with me and report to Lorenzo that I am making a fine recovery."

Consolata moves back toward the writing table to pick up the breakfast tray again when Simonetta continues.

"I am not yet ready to have my breakfast, Consi. I want to talk a while together as we did when we were young girls. I want to remember Marco as he was years ago, when he was my support, my true admirer."

Simonetta waits until Consolata turns toward her to begin.

"1468. So many years ago. When Marco first set eyes on me in Piombino at the signing of our betrothal papers, he was speechless. Even though Piero tried to elicit a few words from him before the signing, he just stood there and smiled. I considered him an imbecile then. A true imbecile. But I could tell I pleased him, and that made me smile in return.

"That day I was convinced everyone present had guessed how uncertain I was, how scared, how timid. I thought my heart had surely betrayed me, it was beating so loudly and so fast. As I looked around, I saw the whole court gathered to give its authority to the alliance. I was cowed. Then when I looked at my mother with her calm demeanor, and Battistina with her radiant smile, I felt greatly reassured. Jacopo was jovial and extremely proud to have made such an advantageous match for our family."

Consolata noticed a mischievous smile playing on Simonetta's lips.

"What are you thinking, my lady?"

"Dear Consi, must you notice every time I have a naughty little thought? Well, then, I must confess. Marco's looks were quite pleasing to me. His grand height, his wavy black hair, his dark eyes, his fair skin made him the most handsome young man. And the slight forward pitch of his skinny torso still reminds me of his constant inclination toward me. Although Piero had arranged our marriage because of my generous dowry, which he insisted should include Elba's iron mines, Marco would have married me even if I had been penniless and an outcast. He called himself my devotee.

"Marco was such a child. His beard had just begun to grow. We were both children. Although I felt much older than my fifteen years, he acted much younger than his. I suspected from the start that we would become the best of friends. I hoped we would tell each other all our secrets and establish between us an easy alliance before the rest of our world. Strangely, even then, I sensed we needed each other's comfort."

Simonetta's smile softens and her expression saddens. Consolata is about to change the subject when Simonetta sighs and continues.

"Had you been able to hide behind the drapes in my bedroom on our wedding night after the official exchange of rings, our anellamento, you would have snickered at the shyness of Marco. It seemed he could not talk to me at all. Only smile.

"When we entered the room together, he touched

my arm, then pulled away as if he had been burnt. He gestured toward the dressing room where you were waiting to help me with my nightgown and then he scuffled across the room to look out the window.

"When he saw me coming toward him as I returned, he stared at me like a simpleton with his mouth open. He was already in bed, his nightshirt on and the covers pulled up to his chest as if he were protecting himself from some invader.

"Once we were alone and I too had settled under the covers, Marco asked if I were comfortable. When I nodded yes, he bent over me, reached for my arm, turned my body to his, and pulled me toward him. Then, he kissed me on the cheek.

"I'm glad you have become my wife." He whispered. He smiled at me again and pulled me closer to him, his eyes full of love and happiness.

"I whispered in his ear, 'You are my husband now. I am praying we will become the best of friends and you will always be my protector.'"

Consolata worries that Simonetta is becoming too tired. She starts toward the bed. Although Simonetta's voice has become almost a whisper, she continues talking.

"Oh, Consi, that first night with Marco I did not know what to expect. I had observed how my mother and Gaspi touched and held each other. They would laugh and tease me about being held and kissed by some strong handsome man. Then they would give each other a little kiss and laugh in a way that made me want to be grown up and a wife right away.

"After all these years, I am still embarrassed by my uncertainty and nervous anticipation of that night. I lay there with my eyes shut, waiting for Marco to react to my words. I could feel his body responding as he held me against him. I did not utter a sound. I did not move but something was happening I had never felt before.

"Quite suddenly, Marco turned away from me without saying a word and lay back on his pillow. For what seemed hours I waited, hardly breathing, not knowing what to do.

"Finally I heard his breath become regular. I knew then he was asleep. I felt as though someone had slapped me. To this day, I never know what to expect of this man who is my husband."

Consolata puts her hand over Simonetta's.

"My lady," she whispers.

Slowly Simonetta closes her eyes and murmurs the same words she had prayed on her wedding night.

Dear God. Please keep my heart pure and help me to love Marco all through my life. Help me to know how to be a good wife to him and guide him to be a good husband. I shall surely need your help. Amen.

As if all her efforts to regain her self composure have failed her, Simonetta begins coughing. Ragged, convulsive sounds. Once the coughing has subsided, Consolata puts her hand forward again, offering Simonetta a handkerchief. Instead of taking the handkerchief, Simonetta grabs Consolata's hand and whispers,

"Oh, Consi, I am so afraid."

8

Simonetta's eyes close almost before she finishes her sentence.

Carefully Consolata arranges the covers over her mistress, picks up the breakfast tray and starts for the door. Before she can exit, Simonetta opens her eyes again.

"Do not leave me, Consi. I need to talk about my first weeks with Marco while I was still on my wedding journey, happy and optimistic. Perhaps if we live through those days again together, I can dispel this blackness I am feeling."

Consolata turns away from the door and sets the tray again on the writing table. She crosses to the opposite side of the room and sits down on the small three-legged chair next to Simonetta's wedding chest in anticipation of the coming monologue. Almost every day lately, Simonetta has retold the story of her marriage and her early days with Marco.

Consolata knows Simonetta's story by heart. First

the betrothal at Piombino where the official agreement to the terms of the dowry, il documento dotale, was signed. Next also at Piombino, the anellamento, followed by a grand wedding feast and the first wedding night. Third, the wedding journey from Piombino to Florence with a stop at Pisa for a few days. And finally, the three days of wedding feasts in Florence at the Vespucci palazzo. Consolata had been with Simonetta for all the events, of course, but she never tires of having Simonetta retell those times they experienced together.

"Please, my lady. I would love to hear you tell the story again."

Consolata rises and helps Simonetta arrange the pillows so that she is leaning comfortably against the wooden backboard of the bed.

Even before Consolata can sit again, Simonetta begins to spill out the oft-repeated words as if some great compulsion has overtaken her.

"In those days when I was on my wedding journey, the world seemed so full of wonders that I lay abed every night beside Marco, awake and examining each day, turning it over and over in my mind like a shiny globe held in my hand.

"I have always been one to ask questions. I know so very little and I question everything. I could barely sleep for there was so much to think about. The changing flora, the rolling fertile land around us which lay fallow, the smell of fire from the chimneys of the cottages we passed. Did the trees provide nuts like the pinoli from home? What was planted in each field in spring? Who lived in each cottage? Were they as happy as we? How many children did they have? All such simple questions, yet so important to me.

"Now I am hounded by more complex questions. Where do the stars come from? Is the world flat or round? How does the soul obtain immortality? What kind of love is pure enough to be divine?"

Simonetta glances at Consolata to be sure she is still listening.

"The first few days of our nuptial journey from Piombino to Florence were spent in Pisa, as you know. Pisa is still the most heavenly of little towns, a glittering jewel of pure marble. Sitting just above the marshland at the entrance to the Arno, it is like a miniature city painted in the background of one of Benozzoti's murals.

"You were not with us when Marco took me to Campo dei Miracoli, the Field of Miracles, on our first day there. The area is well named. The meadow is tended by the priests and planted with a soft green covering whose name I do not remember. I have never since seen a space so flat and begging for people to walk on its paths. The campanile, such a beautiful bell tower, is leaning as it has been since it was first built. I wish you could have seen it. You would have loved to take your folio and pastels and sketch the ornate carvings that ring the surface.

"The cathedral, the bell tower and the baptistery are all magnificent as they sit like intricately carved ivory chess pieces on a board of green. But what impressed me most was Camposanto, the Field of Saints. Locals say its dirt was brought back from the Holy Land during the Crusades and a body will decay within twenty-four hours when it is placed in that dirt. On the field there is a building that is larger than the cathedral itself. Death hovers all around. Black marble memorial stones, each with a carved Angel of Death protruding from it, cover the floor and hang from the walls. These dark figures seem to be waiting in the shadows to claim their next victim."

Before continuing, Simonetta hugs herself as if she has experienced a chill.

"I remember a part of a poem that sprang to my mind as I stood there.

> *Noble men are buried in this sacred soil*
> *Brought back by Crusaders from Golgotha.*
> *Each gravestone has its own dark angel*
> *simple enough for a child to draw*
> *and dream about at night.*
>
> *In daylight, every one of us creates our own disaster,*
> *imagines our own death so many times*
> *that when death comes and is not a game,*
> *without thinking,*
> *we ask the familiar figure in.*

"I had the urge to scream just to hear my voice

resound from the perfectly straight rows of walls. I wanted to assure myself I was not among the dead. How thankful I was for the little bit of color Gozzoli's frescoes gave to some of the walls. Color always reminds me a world of the living still exists.

"I longed then to stay in Pisa until spring so I could smell the blossoming almond trees and watch the crepe myrtles retake their color. How lovely it must be to live in that valley. To be able to look up at Monte Pisanino and dream of riding over those hills bareback.

"My dear, dear Consi. Tell me truly. Do you never tire of hearing me retell this story?"

Consolata straightens her back a little against the stone wall and replies, "Never, Madonna."

Without further persuasion, Simonetta goes on.

"Do you remember? After we left Pisa, we stopped at Cascina for the night. There we heard many tales of the exploits of the Medici in the region, especially in the surrounding hills where they do their hunting and hawking. And of the wars. We couldn't help but be impressed by the degree of fortification around the city. It was difficult to believe that just over one hundred years ago, this village had been the site of one of the most important battles between Pisa and Florence.

"The mistress of the household spoke to us of the spa at the mineral springs in San Giuliano which had been destroyed during another skirmish between Pisa and Florence earlier in the century. She told us how she used to go there with her mother and aunts to take the waters."

Simonetta struggles to suppress the smile that is beginning to inch across her face.

"She also told us about the nearby ancient town of Lucca where there is a beautiful cathedral which is worth the pilgrimage. The Etruscans constructed the wall around the city so thick that a carriage with four horses abreast can ride long the top of it and not come near the sides. So impenetrable, no army can breach it. I had to laugh when she intimated that those walls were built to keep out the Pisan women who found the tall dark-haired Etruscans totally irresistible.

"How I long to go back to Pisa again. Would you like that, Consi? I would love it. Lorenzo and Giuliano have conquered that whole area with their particular brand of charm and I wish we were there with them right now."

Consolata smiles and nods her agreement. The idea does sound delightful to her and she is sure that her mistress would be happy again if only she could be with her Medici friends.

Simonetta pauses barely long enough to draw a breath before she forges on.

"But as we wound our way eastward and away from the Liguria Sea, I could not help feeling a greater and greater sense of loss. I had never been so far away from the sea. Even in Piombino, I could see the boats in the distance as they headed in or out of port. My enthusiasm for this new land was becoming tempered by a creeping homesickness.

But despite this feeling of loss as we wound our way along the Arno inward to Florence, I was full of anticipation for my new life. I was experiencing a duality of feelings, just like the river we were traveling seemed to be two rivers. In many ways, the Arno still reminds me of myself."

"In which ways, my lady?"

"In the way the river can be so contradictory, Consi. Here in Florence it is wide enough to accommodate two large boats passing, but it becomes smaller and increasingly serpentine as it nears the sea. Sometimes when it catches the light, it is sparkling blue while at others times it seems to have no life at all. Those are the times when it just floats along with the same dull brown color. One day it is full and turbulent, sometimes overflowing its banks, causing great floods. And next it looks like a dried up old stream bed.

"So you see. Just like me. One day I seem to be flowing over with life and sparkling from the sun, and the next, I feel as if my life is near its end and my thoughts so impure as to be as brown as the mud."

"But my lady, we who love you do not notice these changes in you. I am sure this perception is the illness talking and the illness will soon be over."

"Oh, I do hope you are correct, Consi. I pray it. In the meantime, I will try to gather courage to face this one day."

"Then, my lady, perhaps it will help to talk of our arrival here in Florence. I do remember it in the greatest of detail and with so many mixed emotions. Please let me tell my version this time!"

Simonetta is delighted that Consi wants to continue the story even though she loves to tell this part as well. She settles back on the pillows and nods to Consolata to go on with the tale. She is smiling in anticipation of Consi's effusive style and her gossipy tendencies.

Consolata begins. "As we approached the town in the early evening, suddenly there was a procession around us larger than I had ever seen in my life. Do you remember that you, our dear departed Anna and I were riding behind Marco? All the dashing young men of Marco's brigata had ridden out to meet him. We were surrounded by men and the three of us nearly fainted to be in the midst of such virility.

"At the head of the men was Signor Vespucci with a few of his most influential friends. Guards on horses whose mantles were decorated with the fleur de lis of Florence accompanied us. Next followed all our men from Piombino and then the servants who were in charge of your wedding cassone. More than a dozen other large chests made of olive wood with bronze hardware carried much finery and many gifts from Signor Appiani, your brother-in-law, as well as your clothing and our household goods. We must have made quite a spectacle!

"And that was only the beginning. When we entered the Carrara gate and approached Piazza Ognissanti, there came a most riotous sound to greet us. From the opening that led to the courtyard of the Vespucci palace, a flourish of music blared. Trumpets, fifes, violins, and coronets all rang out at the same time. The doorway was dressed in a garland of white flowers wrapped in a scarf of white satin. Two banners hung from the upper windows, each in white and each with two entwined gold rings embroidered on them. I had never seen anything so beautiful! There were so many people in attendance that Anna thought it impossible to make our way through the throng.

"The courtyard and interior rooms were aflame with torches even though evening had barely begun. Signor Piero quickly dismounted and started greeting his friends and giving orders to the servants. Soon after, Signor Marco and his friends followed his father's lead, dismounted and handed over their steeds to be taken away by the servants. That night was to be the first night of the three nights of your wedding feast.

"What a scene. You, Anna, and I were nearly overcome with so many men around and with the music blaring and torches being lit everywhere. Do you remember how awkward we felt? We were sitting there on our horses in the middle of a courtyard full of celebrating men, already drinking and joking about their expertise at gratifying women. I had never heard such talk as we heard then.

"Little did we know, in the midst of all this ribaldry, we were simply being required to await the appearance of the noble lady of the household. What a custom! She was obliged to give us an official greeting before we could be dismounted. And the three of us so bedraggled and tired from the journey. I am sure you were mortified, but you kept smiling and appeared, as ever, gracious when you were finally helped down from your horse and led into the house by Madonna Caterina.

"I must say, my lady, that night was the most astonishing of my life. And quite exciting."

"Consi, you have remembered it perfectly. I do believe you tell it even better than I. Please continue."

"Anna and I, as well as the other serving girls, were impressed that Signor Piero had hired so many and the best musicians for your entry and the three banquets. After each meal, lutes and lyres played melodious songs to soothe the ladies.

"In my opinion, my lady, please forgive me, placating the ladies was a necessity since Signor Piero had also hired four dozen of Florence's most handsome serving men and had them dressed in the latest fashion of red leggings and short tunics. The way they pranced about all evening distracted even the most austere of the fairer sex. They had been trained to make the greatest show of each platter, which they carried high above their heads with one hand. The advantage of such a stance became immediately apparent to the ladies present."

"Now, now, Consi! Do stop being impertinent! You know I am not used to such tantalizing innuendos. And especially not while we are speaking of my own wedding feast! I would never want to be accused of approving such prurient thoughts," Simonetta teased. She was nearly laughing out loud.

Consi smiled too to see her mistress so amused.

"I beg your pardon, my lady, for my impudence. Of course, you would never speak of such diversions. But then, I know you well enough to have observed you are quick to exchange the saying for the doing."

Consolata's concern for Simonetta returns.

"Are you tiring, my lady?"

"Perhaps I should rest, dear Consi. I will do my best to forget your titillating tale and store up a little strength for the Maestro's visit this afternoon. However, the next time I need this story told, I will know what to request. You make it so much more enticing than I. I am much too serious about everything that has happened to me. How lovely to have a little levity."

Before Consolata turns to leave, she arranges the bedclothes and pillows again so Simonetta will be more comfortable, and pats her hand almost like a mother. The two of them have been through so much together. She feels heavyhearted at seeing her mistress lying so still and ever so alone in her large bed.

After Consolata leaves the room, Simonetta begins thinking again about that first night she spent at Via Ognissanti. Marco had left the feast early to join the young men of his old brigata to roust around town. In his haste, he had even forgotten to say goodbye. She had retired to her room with Anna and Consi just after Marco left. She had been deserted and yet she could hear the gaiety below which was supposed to be a celebration of her nuptials. The rest of the banquet attendees continued to eat, drink and toast to the couple's health and offspring. How strange. This custom was totally inexplicable to her.

Sleeping alone that night was her first disillusionment as the wife of Marco. She had had so much love to give and she had been desperate to have that love returned.

The third and final evening of the festivities, Marco did not go with the brigata around town. That evening he came to her and made love as he never had before. She felt herself responding to his kisses and to his body against hers. But even as they were making love, a part of her was absent. Something had changed.

9

As Simonetta drifts off to sleep, she is unsure of whether she is beginning to dream or simply willing herself to be with Giuliano in her imagination. She envisions the two of them sitting on the loggia at Careggi while she tells him her memories of their first encounter.

"I cannot stop thinking of 7 February, 1469, the first day I knew that our futures were to be linked forever. That morning the Vespucci house was all astir with the preparations for Lorenzo's tournament. From the first day that Piero was invited to participate, he demonstrated the most extraordinary change in attitude. He marched around the house with the air of some great conqueror. For weeks and weeks his primary occupation was apparel. He spent hours at the tailors and insisted that his doublet and britches be made of the finest velvet that could be found in his warehouse.

"I know you would have laughed, Giuli, if you had seen Piero. The servants told me he stood before the mirror adjusting his cape and cap until they marveled that his legs could still support him. He was cheery at table, talked incessantly about his excellent

jousting skills, just how perfect his posture would be, and every detail of what he would wear. Every time I heard him bragging thus, I wished for many more grand tournaments to keep him in that rarefied mood."

Simonetta becomes more and more engrossed in her reverie.

"Piero had a new dress made for me, a pale pink silk, so different from the bold colors the other women wore. He chose every detail of my ensemble with the greatest care. Luckily for me, I was fair. He did not require me to have my hair lightened or my face scrubbed mercilessly with an abrasive. I had only to sit still for the hairdresser and apply a little white powder to my forehead and nose.

"For those weeks of preparation, Piero talked to me of nothing else except how handsome you were, Giuli. How talented. How all the young ladies of Florence, married or not, were in love with you. How you, not Lorenzo, were the real prize of the tournament. My assignment was clear. I was to fascinate you, to captivate you, to cause you to be hopelessly enamored of me. I was the Vespucci who was to gain your favor and bring honor to the Vespucci family. Bring additional power and prestige to Piero. I was the one who must one day be your Queen of the Tournament."

For only a second, a look of displeasure passes over Simonetta's visage. But as she takes up her story again, she smiles.

"I sent Consolata out that day to learn what news she could. I wanted to know all about the preparations being made around town. She came back with a grand description of the *whole of the Piazza Santa Croce, including the details of how the grandstands were constructed, how fine white sand had been laid over the entire piazza and how the arena had been divided lengthwise with wooden rails to prepare the field. The boxes of the nobles and church dignitaries on the steps of the church Santa Croce were decorated with the most colorful carpets and banners. Consi reported that the so called modest Vespucci box was even more ornate than our receiving room at Borgo Ognissanti. Her descriptions made me more determined than ever to see this event for myself.*

"What an extravagant planner Lorenzo is. Had you not won my heart first, I surely would be abjectly in love with him. In those days, I was exceedingly easy to impress. I could not believe the sumptuous silks, the ermines, the armor, the jewels. The extraordinary expenditures. Lorenzo bragged about how he had spent more than 10,000 gold florins on the decorations of the square alone. All of Florence was trying to count the number of additional florins spent outfitting those joining him before the tournament in the mostra, one of the most flamboyant processions Florence has ever seen.

"Giuli, I will never forget the standard Lorenzo carried. He had ordered it produced by Verrocchio's studio just after your friend Leonardo da Vinci started working there. The figure painted on the silk was Lucrezia Donati, Lorenzo's mistress, standing in a meadow and dressed in the same blue with fleur de lis as Lorenzo had chosen for his own surcoat that day. She was picking laurel, which of course we all knew was supposed to represent Lorenzo. Gold crowns were scattered about her on a field of white and blue.

92

Behind her were the sun and a rainbow to which Lorenzo's motto had been added in gold script, "Le tems revient." "The good times are returning." What fun we both have had laughing about all the symbolism. But fortunately for us, he has made that prediction come true in the most marvelous ways."

Simonetta cannot pull herself away from this excursion into the past. She is where she wants to be, beside Giuliano at a time when the future is ahead of them. She allows herself to continue her imaginings.

"Although everyone of importance was in attendance, I was just beginning to know who the great families were. The Albizzi, the Saltati, the Pazzi, the Pitti, the Pucci, and, of course, the Tornabuonis, your dear mother's family. My mother-in-law had to spend the whole time explaining to me who each family was and why they were so prestigious.

"The Vespuccis sat in a box not far from Lucrezia Donati, who, along with your mother and her attendants, was in the very center box. Ever since Lorenzo had chosen Lucrezia as Queen of the Tournament only a few weeks before his marriage to Clarice, the whole of Florence was speculating about whether or not Lucrezia was his mistress. Some thought she was simply his ideal of Platonic perfection about whom he wrote excellent sonnets. But Consi repeated some of the bawdy songs being sung around town which indicated otherwise in very explicit terms.

"I nearly swooned when Lorenzo, laughing and holding his helmet crowned with a garland of roses and sky-blue feathers, knelt in front of Lucrezia, offering her the silk scarf from around his neck. He rode five different horses during the tournament and *looked the part of a prince for the entire day. What a lot of gossip resulted when he was later given the tournament trophy, a silver helmet encrusted with a golden Mars, even though he had been dismounted twice. Poor Lorenzo. He had had to admit amid the furor that he was not highly skilled with the use of weapons.*

Simonetta feels flushed. Even her remembrances make her react as she did that day. She visualizes Giuli beside her again and looks into his eyes.

"And you, my dear Giuli, oh, my. How handsome you were! Your lively caramel eyes, your tanned face, your thick hair. Your shoulders seemed impossibly broad for one so young. Your frock coat was made of silver brocade strewn with pearls and you sat so very tall in the saddle. A velvet cap adorned with three feathers worked in gold and more pearls and rubies than one could count sat jauntily on your shining auburn curls.

"You seemed full grown. You were still only a boy of fifteen, but to me you were every bit a man.

"Lorenzo rode in front of you astride the horse given to him by the King of Naples. He was resplendent wearing his bejeweled black velvet hat and carrying his shield with three golden fleur de lis, a huge diamond in the middle. But Lorenzo, for all his grandeur, could not compare to you in my eyes.

"Already you had seduced me with your reputation, Giuli. From Piero, I had heard over and over of your skill at riding and throwing, jumping and wrestling, and how you loved the hunt. Among the young women of my acquaintance, you were renowned for your dancing, singing and writing of amorous poetry. That and much, much more. But that day, you beguiled me with your

person. When I added the very real sight of you to all I had heard, I was the one totally enraptured. I was the one ensnared much more firmly than either Piero or I could have predicted."

Simonetta stirs a little and turns to her side. She wills herself to finish her daydream before it fades, leaving her to face the reality of the rest of the day.

"At the very moment when you stopped before the Vespucci box, smiled, bowed and looked directly into my eyes, hesitating a bit longer than was proper, promising more than I had ever imagined one could promise with only a glance, I gave my heart away forever. I could see my own reflection in your eyes and could tell by the flare of joy and mischief in yours that you were as captivated as I. I was yours then as I am now. I have been from that very second. Should we be immortal, my love for you will never become less consuming. One glance. One word. One glimpse across a room. Passion aflame again."

10

Several hours later, Simonetta sits down on the chair which Consolata had placed in the middle of the room. She is exhausted. She has tolerated Maestro Stefano's many questions and has coughed each time he asked her to so that he can evaluate the condition of her lungs. In addition to the trial of having to comply with all his directives during the examination, she was forced to drink a disgusting concoction in front of him. The whole ordeal was very tiring.

Now that the doctor has taken his leave, Simonetta is faced with the business of undressing again and putting on her everyday clothes. All this activity has taxed her so that she is still resting on the chair when Consolata hastens into the room with a letter Piero has written and the news of the courier's imminent arrival.

Simonetta reads the letter over quite rapidly. She can hardly contain her joy when she reads the words, "She is rather better…" in Piero's report to Lorenzo about Maestro

Stefano's findings.

"Consi, I am so relieved. Maestro Stefano says I am better. I can't wait to write the news to Giuliano before the courier arrives today. Please, Consi, hurry and bring me my supplies."

As Consi leaves the room, Simonetta is already immersed in her own thoughts.

How puzzling. Piero has sent Consolata with a letter that he is about to post to Lorenzo. He must have an ulterior motive. Possibly he wants me to learn what the doctor had to say from a letter rather than coming to see me himself. Then again, he may want to impress upon me how much this doctor is charging and how he, Piero, is forced to hint to Lorenzo to help him pay a part of it. The latter motive seems more like Piero to me.

Whatever the reason, I have no time to waste. I need to prepare my letter to Giuliano immediately. The courier usually passes by about four in the afternoon and it is already past two.

Simonetta stands, walks over to her writing table and sits down again. As she does so, she forces herself to focus her thoughts on what she will write to Giuliano once Consolata has returned with her supplies.

Memories, daydreams, visions, nightmares. These have been my life recently. But not for long. Soon I will be well. I will once again walk with Consolata down the Via del Porcellana to stroll the gardens of Santa Maria Novella and admire, as always, the intricate design of the church's facade. If I am feeling very strong, I might spend some time inside the church looking at the newly finished painting by my friend Sandro, yet another one called

Adoration of the Magi. *Perhaps I will even be strong enough to walk to the Ponte alla Carraia where I can cross my beloved Arno and head up into the hills beyond the lovely Santo Spirito church.*

When Consolata returns with the little chest containing Simonetta's paper, ink, and pen, along with her seal and sealing wax, Simonetta cannot stop herself from blurting out, "Oh, Consi. I am so happy! I do think I might burst with happiness! Did you hear the words of the doctor? There is hope! Hope that I will soon feel like myself again. Hope that I can go again to the Medici palace on Via Largo and be there with Giuli, walking in the gardens or stealing away to a private corner. Or sit with Lucrezia on the loggia overlooking the garden. Or spend time with Lorenzo in his large study beside the Great Hall. I can debate with my friends of the Accademia. Talk of poetry. There is no end to the things I want to do again.

"When I think of Via Largo, I always think of Giuliano first. But from time to time I do think of the many amusing hours I have spent with Lorenzo in his grand studiolo. There is enough space in that room for more than a dozen of his retinue to sit on the ornately carved benches that line the walls, but frequently I am the only one whom he invites."

With a smile both wise and resigned, and more than a little radiant, Simonetta thinks of one day early in her friendship with Lorenzo when he had persuaded her to follow him into his study. She had been a little hesitant, not because she was afraid, but because she was so willing.

Lorenzo waited at the door for me and stood with his back against the jamb so I was forced to suck in my breath as I passed him, my breasts barely brushing his tunic as I entered.

"Giuliano will be jealous," he teased. Although his eyes followed me across the room, he did not move from the stance he had assumed in the doorway until I sat before his writing table on the Florentine folding chair reserved for his special guests.

Lorenzo crossed the room and seated himself behind his writing table, his eyes focused on the objects there the whole time. As if to regain the composure he seemed to have lost, he picked up a folio of paper and his quill pen.

Slowly he looked up at me.

"So, my dear girl. What is this I hear about you and my little brother?"

His mouth had asked a simple question, but his eyes were full of anguish and yearning. No one had ever looked at me so intently.

Before I could answer, Lorenzo looked down again at the folio he held in his hand.

"My brother seems most taken with you." he continued. "Not unlike every man in my court, as you must know. Provoked by your beauty and grace. I speak for myself as well. However I gather Giuliano is the one who has stolen your heart."

Lorenzo stopped as if someone had put a gag in his mouth. Looking as if he might actually choke, he sat down his pen and folio and extended his hand slowly across the table, meeting my eyes. I carefully stretched out my hand too until he could cover it with his own. I was so overcome with emotion, I did not know *what to do or think.*

After several seconds, Lorenzo lowered his eyes, turned without a word and took down the birth tray he had brought me there to see. The spell was broken, but the fervor remained.

When Simonetta emerges from her remembering and looks again at Consolata, Consi has a strange expression on her face. She is wondering which scene from the past Simonetta is replaying in her mind this time.

Without acknowledging Consolata's quizzical look, Simonetta continues.

"I remember the day Lorenzo took me alone to his studiolo with the sole purpose of showing me his birth tray. Of all the precious objects he has collected and keeps there, I do believe he loves this desco da parto the most. Florentines will spend a fortune in florins to have an ornate tray prepared for the birth of a child. And Lorenzo's is truly as magnifico as il Magnifico himself.

"How he would laugh to hear me say such a thing. Very disrespectful, wouldn't you say, Consi?"

"I would say that being disrespectful is not a behavior that comes hard to either one of us, Madonna. And what would you answer to that accusation?"

Simonetta smiles at her friend's teasing, but ignores her question and continues.

"I find the whole custom charming. Lucrezia once told me the trays are commissioned to honor the mother and are used to serve her delicacies after she has given birth. Lorenzo's is said to be the largest and most precious of all the birth trays ever created. I was astonished when I first saw it. It is a meter in diameter and has the most detailed painting with scenes from the works of both Boccaccio and Petrarch. There can be no question as to why it is called *The Triumph of Fame*. At the time Piero de' Medici commissioned Guidi to execute the birth plate, he like his father, Cosimo, was determined that the Medici family would be the most famous ever to control the Republic of Florence.

"Oh, my. Here I am extolling Lorenzo's birth tray when I should be about writing to Giuli. But Consi, I long to be served delicacies from a tray made for my own son. I have waited, wished and prayed that I would be blessed with a child. The midwives say that my time will come, as you do, but I am not so certain. Should I ever be blessed with a child, I hope it will be Giuliano's, not Marco's.

Simonetta startles. She has shocked not only herself, but Consolata by what she has just uttered.

"You must tell no one what I have just said, Consi. No one. Do not let even a hint escape. Promise me, Consi."

"Of course, I promise, my lady. I have never given away even the smallest of your secrets. I have never even intimated how you can sit for hours before your tabernacle mirror, a mysterious smile on your face. Surely if I can keep that little secret of yours, you can trust me to the death to keep this most intimate of secrets. I will never tell. Not even under torture."

Simonetta relaxes a little.

"Lucrezia says that Lorenzo's wife grows more

beautiful with each child. I am convinced the partum does not cause this change, but the fact that Lorenzo spends more and more of his nights with the family. Marco has told me he often drinks and sups with the brigata, but then returns to the palace before the young men start their carousing. At Careggi, I have seen him leave his friends when they are hoping to discuss philosophy or poetry with him to go play with the children. Or have the children come to him. Clarice must be very happy. No wonder she grows more beautiful."

Simonetta frequently thinks of Clarice, who has already borne Lorenzo three children. She has never forgotten how Clarice, her red hair billowing behind her like a sail and her white silk dress wafting gently on the June breeze, rode down Via Largo on Falsamico, Lorenzo's most magnificent white stallion. She was surrounded by the impressive entourage of fifty cavaliers Giuliano had taken with him to Rome to accompany her back to Florence. She carried herself like a queen, and so she should have, coming from such a great Roman family as the Orsini. Nothing has ever compared to the fanfare and splendor of her entry into her wedding feast.

Practically the whole town followed the wedding party into the palazzo, which had been decorated with garlands of olive branches in all the windows. A whole olive tree had been lifted into the central window and set up there on the balcony of the inner courtyard to give the blessings of plenty and fertility to the young couple.

"My mother says women are their most beautiful

after they have reached their twenty-fifth year. Perhaps in two years when we are both over twenty-five and have babies of our own, we will be twice as beautiful as ever, once for the age and once for the babies."

"My lady, what a thing to say! You are beautiful now. I cannot imagine that you could be more so. I, unfortunately, could use a little improvement."

"Now, Consi. Stop your teasing. I must finish my letter to Giuliano before the courier arrives. Piero would never allow him to wait."

Simonetta regards Consolata with an enigmatic smile.

"My letter must have such warm words that Giuli will be desperate to come back to me, to take me in his arms and give me the child I long for. What do you think of that, Consi?"

"How you do carry on, my lady. I am never sure whether I must take you seriously or not. But I have no doubt your words can entice him to hurry back to you."

As Simonetta turns back to her letter, she cannot stop herself from revisiting old guilts. Her love of Giuliano has also been a betrayal of Marco and an even greater sin before God. How she has transgressed!

Even as she acknowledges her trespasses, she confirms her determination.

I will not give up my longing for Giuliano. I will not give it up even if it condemns me to Hell.

11

My most beloved Giuliano, my great and treasured friend for all time,

I feel like a girl again. I am as excited as I was the first time I was permitted to mount a horse by myself. Today I feel that same sense of freedom and joy for I have received news that my recovery has begun. If only I will follow Maestro Stefano's advice and drink his horrid pharmacies, I shall soon be myself again.

When you return, I will be able to go to Careggi with you. I dream of it constantly. I imagine the two of us standing together on the hillside at the far end of the gardens. We are looking down into the valley and seeing the silhouette of Florence against the backdrop of the far hills. Enjoying the scent of the orange blossoms all around us. Just being with you will be more than I can bear of ecstasy. My exhilaration is almost as great as I felt when we met for the second time at Lorenzo's marriage feasts.

Do you remember how splendid the feasts were? The tables were piled high with trays of sweet meats, marzipan, jellies and sugared pine nuts. The rumor was that one hundred and fifty calves were served, two thousand brace of capons and too many casks of wine to count, many of them imported from France. I was seated at the bride's table with Clarice and fifty or more young noblewomen. Clarice looked radiant. But it was your face I see most clearly now. So long ago and yet I shall forever remember how your face lit up at your first sight of me.

Those three days were among the happiest of my life. I still cherish every moment. Lorenzo was confident and self-possessed, the ideal for a prospective head of state. And so handsome in his unique way. I think it was his strong sense of self that made him appear older, stronger and wiser than his nineteen years would indicate. And although Lorenzo was not yet twenty and you were barely sixteen, the two of you had been called upon to be the representatives of your father while he was ill. And you executed your duties to perfection. I learned more about the ways of princely conduct in those three days than I could have learned in decades from the most instructive of tutors. I still can hardly believe my good fortune to be an honored guest.

I will never forget my first glimpse of you as you entered the courtyard. I felt I was seeing someone I had seen over and over again in my dreams. You fairly swung into the room with a jauntiness that belied your position as second to your brother. All eyes turned toward you as Lorenzo continued to carry on the proprieties that were expected of him.

You were tall, with your torso bent slightly forward, but with the stature and bearing of a true prince. Your lively face was so animated that it almost seemed to precede you into the room. You had a smile that radiated joy, knowledge, power in just the smallest movement of your lips. Your hair was curly, almost chestnut, and like every other part of you seemed to have a life of its own. I could not stop myself from wanting to touch each strand, to take each curl and let it wrap around my fingers with a momentum of its own.

I could not take my eyes off of you at your table where you were laughing and drinking with Lorenzo and his friends. And yet anytime you began to incline toward me, I quickly averted my eyes so that you could never see me trying to seek you out.

You were very clever in your ways as well. No one would have guessed that you were stealing glances at me. Nor would I have, had I not been so captivated by you. I could not be content to look anywhere else for the rest of the evening. How could I return to the innocence and childlike excitement I had felt earlier in the evening? I was forever changed, as if my former self had died and an unknown self had awakened in a new world. I needed God to forgive my total intoxication at merely looking on you again. May the Lord have mercy on my soul, I could not even sustain one prayer to ask for His forgiveness.

The festivities continued into the night and the next morning. And again the next day. And again. What revelry, what music, what dancing! Nothing since has compared with those three days of celebration. To my surprise, I never tired of the music, the dancing, the uproar from jesting and celebratory speeches.

Yes, finally, I will confess to watching you for all three days, being aware of when you got up from table, of those who were standing around you, of how much you were joking with Angelo Poliziano and Marsilio Ficino under the archways, of which of the dancing girls you admired the most. From time to time, you or Angelo would come to the center of the courtyard and signal for all to be silent. Then you would read one of your love poems to the newlyweds and the hall would resound with applause.

Even without searching you out among the others, I could tell when you were watching me. My skin burned, my cheeks reddened. I was truly a maiden again, feeling as I did with my first attraction to a boy.

106

Feeling the same incredible pull toward you I had felt that first day at Lorenzo's joust. Only stronger and more overwhelming.

From that first night of feasts I began to contrive a plan for our meeting. Of course, all my scheming and dreaming could never have prepared me for our actual encounter. I was helpless.

You came bounding down the grand stairs just as I turned the corner below to start up. I could not even bear to glance toward the noise of your footsteps on the marble which was warning me where you were. You, not Lorenzo, nor Poliziano, nor Botticelli, nor any of the others, but you. My prize to be. Your enthusiasm, your lively energy, your quick and agile movement.

As I mounted step by step, all my calculations, all my carefully chosen words went spilling down behind me. I could not lift my eyes. My head remained bowed. Since I needed to pull my skirt up in front, I had to feel for each riser with my foot before I could be assured of my balance. I have never again been so shaky or disconcerted.

You did not seem to notice. You did not seem to notice anything except that I was coming closer to you. Your body surged with the energy of ten young men. When I finally regained my composure and the courage to look up at you, you said nothing. You did not move toward me nor I toward you. You simply reached out your left hand and took my right hand in yours, turned and headed back up the steps towards the chapel at such a gallop I could hardly keep pace.

As you pulled me into the chapel behind you that day, every nerve in my body was strung so tight I thought I might fly apart in a million pieces. The intensity of the colors, the ornamentation of the columns painted like the marble inlaid floors, the sumptuous depictions in Gozzoli's fresco of The Journey of the Magi, all the marvels of this jewel-like chapel were nothing compared to the wonderment I was feeling inside.

You were pointing out the personages who were in the painting; your father, your grandfather, the Pulci brothers, Marsilio Ficino, Lorenzo, and, of course, you. You wore a blue tunic and cap as you sat up proudly astride your horse with your pet cheetah riding behind you. I could see how handsome you were, even as a small boy.

I stood as if struck by lightning while you continued talking as if you thought someone might enter at any moment and find you being the perfect guide. As you circled around me, you were so close I could hear your breath and feel your heat. I was struggling to contain my impulses.

Suddenly, perhaps startled by a noise from below, we both realized where we were and you took me by the hand again. I turned to face you. As I looked up into your eyes, your spirited, searching eyes, I silently pledged, may God forgive me, to love you for all eternity.

As we walked out onto the landing at the top of the stairs, you turned to me, lifted my face to yours and gently brushed my lips with yours. I felt a burning so intense, I do not remember how I stayed upright or how I negotiated the stairs even with your arm supporting mine. I do not remember the rest of the feast. I was as a woman finding my way through a swirl of sounds and objects while my feet barely touched the ground.

My most precious Giuliano, I do not want to end this letter. In writing it, I can relive many of our happiest moments. I can have you with me. I can dream of our next meeting. But soon the courier will pass, so I will send this letter on its way with all my prayers for your safe return.

My esteem and affection to our Lorenzo.

Yours by love possessed, Simonetta,
Via Borgo Ognissanti
20 April 1476

12

Simonetta startles at the sound of Consolata on the stairs.

Consi must be fairly bounding up two at a time Simonetta thinks to herself. Suddenly aware that the letter she has newly finished is waiting to be posted, she admonishes herself for being consumed by her imaginings rather than the business at hand.

"Consi! Consi!"

"I am here, my lady." Consi bursts through the door like a young child. "The courier has not yet come, but he is due any minute."

"Then please hurry, Consi. I certainly do not want to miss him. I have been writing for much longer than I had planned. The sealing wax is dry so you can take it right away. Just be sure to wait for the courier and put the letter directly into his hands. And try to intercept any correspondence for me before Giorgio gets it."

Simonetta hands the letter to Consolata. Although

she is smiling, her mind has wandered back to Giuliano. She prays the courier will be carrying a letter from Giuli today. It has been days since she has heard from him and she longs for word of his exploits. She wants to hear of his unhappiness at not being with her.

"I do wish I were with him, Consi."

"I know, my lady. I know. It will not be long now. And maybe there will be a letter today."

"Has Marco returned these past two nights?"

"I do not know about Signor Marco, Madonna. I wish I had heard more news about him or anyone else to share with you. But with il Magnifico gone and Signor Giuliano with him, there is little happening here in Florence. When I go today to the Ciompi fish market, I will inquire about news from Pisa. There is always some little scrap of gossip from the fish mongers. Usually, though, not enough to be amusing."

"Go then, my dear Consi. Take the letter, but remember to take care not to let Piero or that secretary of his have it in hand. Wait by the door for the courier to arrive, then go and hand it to him directly. I do not want Piero to know my intimate thoughts or what anguish I suffer when Giuliano is absent."

"Do not fret, Madonna. I will do exactly as you ask."

"I trust you, Consi. You are a very clever young woman and much more worldly than I despite all my pretenses. Hurry, now, before it is too late. I will be waiting impatiently for your return."

The brush of Consolata's linen skirt on the stones as she turns and marches toward the door reminds Simonetta of her own desire to rise and move to the window. There she will be able to observe Consi with the courier and will be assured that he received her letter to Giuliano without interference. A faint smile appears on her pale lips.

Perhaps there really will be a letter from Giuli today.

Without being aware of her actions, Simonetta replaces her quill and paper in the cassetta. Her supply of parchment is almost gone again after only a few days. She will be forced to appeal to Piero for more. He will be more curious than ever about this constant need for more paper, but she will be able to assure him it is for her poetry and her other writings, which he, thank goodness, takes no interest in seeing.

I have always been able to divert Piero's attention and make him smile. Although he has never approached me again in the same way he did on that day he gave me the pearls, I am sure he has always been a bit in love with me. Perhaps he still sometimes imagines himself in Marco's or Giuliano's place in my affections. Of course, he would never admit to his folly because of his position and his vanity.

I came to this household as a young bride and now I am in full womanhood. And yet there has been no child. How I have prayed. Is God punishing me? How can I feel fulfilled with no babe to hold in my arms? With no son to protect me. No adoring face of a young daughter to reflect back my own face. Try as I may not to think about my loss, there are times when my arms ache to hold a child. When my breasts begin to feel swollen and sensitive.

Suddenly Simonetta finds she is rocking back and forth as though she is holding that child tight against her and singing a lullaby to soothe him. She stands up from her writing table and glances toward the door.

Sometimes my loneliness is so great, I would welcome the boisterous sound of Marco running up the stairs to my room, teasing all the maids he encounters on the way. Marco can always act the affable lighthearted young man whose affairs sit effortlessly on his shoulders.

Today I would be content to sit quietly in front of him and have him tell me of his exploits. Or how the officials continue to argue over the same laws almost every day at the Signoria. Or what new marvel is being hawked at the mercato. Anything would do. Marco can tell a very entertaining story. He has had much practice because Piero used him to help charm the foreign courts whenever he was sent abroad by Lorenzo.

The sound of a bell from one of the gurneys that are constantly going to and from Santa Maria dell'Umiltà, the charity hospital next door, brings Simonetta back to reality. She turns from her chair and moves across the floor with surprising ease. As she climbs up the steps to the window, she thinks of the suffering so many in this city are forced to endure. She can hardly bear to think of the poor beings constantly being carried into the hospital moaning in great distress, and then more often than not, being carried out again, still and cold.

As she looks down the street to her left, Simonetta sees a woman with a huge belly lying on a gurney. She is dressed in the coarsest jute. Simonetta cannot be sure of her age, but only that she is in great pain so that her cries echo from building to building along the narrow street. Simonetta feels a sudden chill as she thinks of this woman's anguish. Many women come to the hospital when there is a problem with the birthing of their babies. By the time they arrive, however, it is usually too late.

Simonetta has never visited this hospital that the Vespucci family helped build, although several times she has been invited to accompany Anastasio, Marco's uncle and the grandson of Simone who founded the charity. Her own mother surely would have gone had she had the chance. Catocchia is generous and compassionate. Simonetta has always wished she were more like her mother in these respects.

Guido Antonio, another of Marco's uncles, a judge who also is reputed for his benevolence, always takes a special interest in Simonetta. He flatters her each time he comes to visit and she is often invited to dine with his family even though Caterina and her sisters-in-law are seldom asked. Guido Antonio is the one who chose Simonetta as the Madonna who watches over the family in the fresco that Anastasio commissioned for the Vespucci chapel next door in the Church of the Ognissanti.

Simonetta is still flattered by his choice. She loves the innocent and protective look Ghirlandaio gave her when he executed the painting. In the fresco, which he calls *Madonna della Misericordia*, the Madonna of Mercy, she looks even younger than she did at fifteen when she first came to Florence. Two angels help hold her cape out directly from her shoulders as the entire Vespucci family kneels beneath it, surrounding her. The grandparents, Amerigo and Nonna, are on each side of her long full skirt. The rest of the family are gathered around them, even young Amerigo, Marco's cousin who later went to Spain seeking adventure as an explorer to the New World.

Simonetta glances down to the right toward the entryway of Ognissanti, her church, where the penitents are entering for confession. How long has it been since she has gone to confession? Many weeks. Perhaps she will go again today. As soon as Consolata returns.

Surely she must have the strength for such a little exertion as descending the center stairs, walking through the courtyard, turning west for only a few steps and entering her dear little church. Not so much strength would be required for that. The doctor says she is getting stronger and she must build her stamina for Giuliano's return. If she begins to exert herself right away, she will be ready if he arrives sooner than expected.

A noise below in the courtyard draws her attention away from her musings and she sees the courier dismount his horse. Consolata is waiting, as is Giorgio, Piero's secretary who is in charge of all household correspondence. Had Simonetta not appealed to Piero to let Consolata handle her correspondence, Giorgio would have insisted that he be the one to be in charge of her letters.

Watching the courier and Giorgio together amuses Simonetta. Always, Giorgio walks straight forward toward the courier in the most formal of postures. He stops about ten feet away and waits patiently for the courier to dismount and come to him. Of course Giorgio insists the courier comes to him so it is clear who is in the superior position. Long ago Simonetta had learned that trick at the court in Piombino. She uses it even now from time to time herself.

Piero's pretentious secretary waits until the courier bows and straightens. Then he watches carefully as the courier takes a series of letters, folded and properly sealed with wax, from the crude leather satchel hanging around his neck. Next he hands them to Giorgio.

Slowly Giorgio examines each letter to be sure the wax seal has not been broken and the parchment is still undamaged. Then he puts them in the black embossed leather portfolio that he carries with him always. It is his badge of importance. Next he pulls from the portfolio just one letter and with great formality hands it to the waiting man, stating his instructions in a modulated voice.

Simonetta wonders if that letter might be the same one Piero had sent her to read, but she has every reason to believe it is instead about other business. Something about Giorgio's intimate mutterings indicate this letter does not have the pompousness that accompanies any letters Piero might send to il Magnifico.

Giorgio pulls a coin from his pocket and holds it out to the courier, who takes it and bows again. While he is still bowing, Giorgio turns on his heels and heads back into the house.

Only after the secretary disappears does Consolata step forward. The courier smiles for the first time as she advances toward him. He quickly holds out his hand for Simonetta's letter and bends to hear Consolata's instructions as if the two of them were conspirators in some faraway place.

Simonetta breathes a sigh of relief that her letter is in trustworthy hands. All at once, a fatigue comes over her that makes her wish for her bed. Instead she seats herself on the chair beside the window and tries to make her breath come easily and regularly once more.

Before she can regain her normal breathing rhythm, there is a tap on the door.

"Enter," Simonetta calls. When she rises to move toward the door, she is not sure whether her heart is fluttering in hopes that someone is bringing her a letter from Giuliano or if she is simply still out of breath.

Abruptly, someone slams the door against the wall. It is full open. Giorgio is standing there with an air of expectation, a letter in his hand. She recognizes his ploy. He is hoping that she will rush toward him to receive the letter so that he may feel his power. But she is in no mood to play games this afternoon. She simply repeats, "Enter." She remains standing upright in the middle of the room.

116

Giorgio has no choice but to move across the room toward her. His expression is severe, even more so than usual. He does not like to be the one who is manipulated. Like so many other less important officials, he likes to control each minute movement so he can increase his carefully constructed perception of his own importance.

As he advances toward her, Simonetta holds out her right hand to receive the letter which Giorgio is still holding close to his cloak.

"Signor Vespucci has asked me to bring this letter to you. It is a letter from someone important within the Medici family. It bears the Medici seal."

"Thank you, Giorgio. You are most kind. Please tell Signor Vespucci I will read it at my convenience and will send for him if there is something of importance he must know."

Simonetta is quite aware that she is not giving Giorgio the satisfaction he is seeking, nor is she revealing her own elation that a letter of such importance should arrive for her. It pleases her to be able to exercise control of her emotions despite the fact that she is so full of anticipation.

Giorgio, of course, does not bow. He simply says, "As you wish, Madonna. I will relay your message to Signor Vespucci." Then he turns and walks directly through the unclosed door, leaving it open for Simonetta to close.

Simonetta quickly crosses the room, closes the door and picks up her letter opener from the writing table, eager to know who has sent this letter.

13

To catch more light, Simonetta pulls her chair closer to the window. After she sits, she cautiously uses the letter opener to pry open the seal, trying not to mar the paper but still keep the seal intact. She knows this is not a letter from Lorenzo or the courier would have told Giorgio it was from Pisa. And Giuliano uses a different color of wax. No, this must be from another member of the Medici family. Clarice, perhaps, or even Lucrezia herself.

Unfolding the several sheets of paper, Simonetta reads:

Most esteemed and honorable Simonetta,

Surely you must be surprised to receive a missive from me when I am rarely in communication with you outside of our delightful encounters in the country at Careggi or here at Via Largo when my sons are in town. Although I am frequently in correspondence with your esteemed father-in-law about the business of the Republic, you are right to wonder as to the nature of this letter written directly to you.

There really is no mystery herein. The simple truth is, I am at this moment writing you at Lorenzo's request. He wishes you to know that he has received the letter from Piero dated April 18 regarding the precarious condition of your health. As soon as Lorenzo shared the news, Giuliano determined he would leave his affairs in Pisa and come directly to Florence to call upon you himself as soon as possible. He wishes to discern in person the state of your health. He should be arriving within the next few days.

Maestro Stefano has informed me upon my recent inquiry that you are much improved and that he has great hopes for your total recovery. I am praying everyday to Our Lady that he is right and you will soon be joining us at Via Largo or Careggi. All of us have sorely missed your reassuring presence.

Lorenzo informs me that you ask frequently about my health. I thank you for your concern. I am pleased to report that for an old lady and one suffering from acute arthritis at that, I am doing quite well in these spring months. I did not even need to go to the spas this past winter, despite the damp and cold. Perhaps it is because Lorenzo keeps me so busy with the affairs of the Republic that I have little time to think of myself.

The task of being in charge while he is away is particularly occupying as I must hear the petitions of all who come to Via Largo. And as you may guess, in these trying times, there are many. One would think I should be exhausted from the exertion. But I am convinced what tires me most at present is missing my two sons and their friends such as yourself. The house is devoid of frivolity and intellectual challenge when none of you are here.

During this lack of external stimulation, I apply myself even more diligently to my writing. Poliziano has graciously offered to review my Storie Sacre *as soon as he returns from Pisa so that I may be assured that they are written in perfect terzinas. He has also taken it upon himself to read my latest poems, so I anxiously await his opinion. We Florentines are so fortunate to have had a precursor of such merit as Dante who gave us many fine examples of style and form. How I wish I were able to capture in my own poetry the beauty and portent of his.*

I trust you have been feeling strong enough during your illness to continue your studies and writings. Your poetry has originality and naturalness which I find lacking in my own, especially when I write of Biblical personages. I would be most honored to read some of your latest poems, should you wish to share them with me. I have great respect for your perceptions and the innovations with which you express them.

I am more and more convinced that we women with unrelenting minds who have been given the advantage of good educations and supportive men must see that our daughters and granddaughters as well as those of our friends have the same opportunity to study and express themselves as we have had. I am honored to sit among the members of the Accademia as an esteemed equal in matters of the mind. Cosimo, my wise and generous father-in-law, often spoke to me of how he wished that women could play a greater role in the Republic. I consider myself fortunate to have known him and to have been the recipient of his astute considerations.

Although the joys of my life are great, the obligations of being the matriarch of such an eminent family leave me much less time for contemplation or writing than I would wish. I have the supplications and disputes left to me by Lorenzo to resolve in addition to overseeing and provisioning the multitudinous households and plantations we own. I also see to the education of all who are a part of our properties. Of course, as always, I consider my most sacred duty is to attend to the spiritual

120

requirements of our family and household members.

I praise the Lord every day that I am ever blessed with the strength to perform these venerable obligations given me through little merit of my own. I gain much satisfaction in doing so and great joy in thinking that, as my sons tell me, I am not only widely loved but highly regarded.

I am forever grateful for your gentle and loving presence in my life and the lives of my family. I am especially appreciative for the considerable influence you have on Giuliano.

Please commend me to your father-in-law. I shall be in communication with him soon. And should you wish to write to me personally, I would be most honored to receive your letter.

Along with my prayers for the safety of Lorenzo and Giuliano while they are away from us, I pray several times daily to Our Lady for your continued recovery. May God grant you His blessings. Peace be with you in these difficult days.

Yours in Christ,
Lucrezia de' Medici
Via Largo
20 April 1476

Part III

22 April 1476

Magnifico, I present myself to you, your honorable compatriot,

In these past days I have written you of Simonetta's improvement; however, her illness has not gone as I believed it would, nor as would have been our desire. This evening there has been a dispute between Maestro Stefano and Maestro Moyse in trying to arrive at a conclusion of what medicine should be given, and this medicine they have given her. I cannot yet see what good it has done. God alone can do what we want done.

And because the last time I wrote you about the discomfort I felt in the reimbursement and salary of M. Stefano, and since you have not responded, I have not known how to pay either, and for eight days it has been on my conscience, and now at this point we must see who we must follow. Although no one has told me the illness is terminal, without this being the case, our intention is this: it would be very dear of you to send us a few words with your opinion. (Please know that Simonetta has again the symptoms of fever, vomiting, coughing, insomnia, and lack of appetite. We have so many other doctors here in Florence who could be called, principally among them, Dietifeci Ficino, the father of Marsilio. I hesitate to do so as I have not heard from you, nor from Marco, nor Giuliano, nor others of her family who are concerned in the matter. Not even Catocchia, her mother, has offered suggestions or made a move to come from Piombino to be in charge of her ill and perhaps dying daughter.)

These two doctors are suffering from their own discord. M. Stefano says it is not consumption and M. Moyse says just the opposite; I don't know who is the better to follow.

Florence, 22 April 1476.
I commend myself to you, Piero Vespucci

14

As I bow before the Crucifix suspended above the altar at *Il Duomo, Santa Maria del Fiore*, I notice a beam of light from *Brunelleschi's* dome reflecting off the marble floor like a crown of prisms. Around me the rest of the massive cathedral hangs in hazy gloom. I cross myself then rise to follow *Caterina* and my sisters-in-law into the family pew on the right. *Piero* sits beside me on the end nearest the center aisle. He seems somewhat nervous and extraordinarily alert to all that is going on around him.

From our position several pews back from the front row where the *Medici* sit, I can see *Lorenzo* enter the *Canonic* door on the right with *Angelo Poliziano* and several other friends. They stand in the shadows, continuing to chat and laugh even after the mass has begun. I cannot see *Giuliano* from where I am sitting, but I can hear a commotion from the left side of the apse as he enters the *Almond* door with *Francesco de' Pazzi* and *Bernardo Bandini*. *Giuli's* friends are laughing and prancing about him even though the choir has begun singing. Their puppet-like movements are all quickly ended as *Giuliano* seeks out his place to the left of the altar.

Searching for another glimpse of Giuliano, I see the glint of a knife in the distance. I am sure it is a dagger. My reaction is swift this time. I do not wait for it to descend, but scream and surge upright almost to a standing position.

As she pitches forward, Simonetta realizes she is still in her bed. She throws off the covers and calls for Consolata, trying to make her voice sound as normal as possible.

Simonetta has become accustomed to these nightmares which occur several times every night. Each night her understanding of what is happening becomes clearer. Although some of the details have changed with each dream, there is always the glint of a knife held high. There is always extreme fear. Always, too, she awakes shaking and drenched in sweat.

"Consolata. Come quickly. I feel painfully cold." Her voice is so low as she finishes the sentence that she wonders if she has even said it aloud.

"My lady, my lady, I am here. I am here now." Consolata calls as she rushes into the room without knocking. "Have you had another nightmare? You will surely need some hot stones and broth to help you regain your warmth. I will ask one of the servants to fetch them."

"Please, Consi, I do not want to alarm the rest of the household. What helps me most is to have you near. Your presence comforts me. I need you to sleep in the trundle bed until I get better. If you are here beside me, I can wake you with only a whisper."

"Of course, my lady."

"Do not leave me, Consi. Ever. You are my greatest comfort in this house. Promise. Promise you will never leave me while I am in this house."

"I promise you, my lady. I promised your mother I would always look after you and be a mother and sister to you as best I can. But be assured this promise weighs lightly on me, for there is nowhere I would rather be than beside you. Now you must rest, my lady. Please lie back and let me pull your covers over you. You can tell me just a little of what you have dreamt."

"No, Consi. I do not want to talk about these nightmares. God is punishing me by making me have these frightful visions where Giuliano is in great danger. He is punishing me with fear for the safety of the one I love most. That is how he is telling me that I must rid myself of this impurity."

Consolata waits patiently for Simonetta to recover her composure.

"Please, Consi, go and fetch my breakfast tray. When you return we will talk of pleasant things. But first, open the shutters for me so I can look out on Bellosguardio Hill and hear the bells of Santo Spirito."

Simonetta lies back on her damp pillows as Consolata crosses the room, goes up the steps before the window and pulls the shutters back to each side. Simonetta had not risen from her bed the day before, so this is the second time in as many days that Consolata has been requested to open the shutters. Piero has sent for both doctors to come today. He is much afraid that Simonetta is not making the progress they predicted or he had hoped.

As Consolata softly closes the door, Simonetta is already beginning to hear the music which was played for the ball of Eleanora d'Aragon. That ball was a grand affair given in Eleanora's honor over three years ago when she stopped at Florence on her way to marry Ercole d'Este in Ferrara. Simonetta can still see the dozens of torches which illuminated the great courtyard of the Palazzo della Signoria. She remembers the festoons of flowers everywhere. The whole scene was enchanting.

As Simonetta continues to reminisce, she recalls how Piero had spent much of his time for weeks prior to the ball being sure that Simonetta would appear dressed and coiffed to "best show off her assets." At least those were his words. He had wanted her to impress Alfonso, the heir to the throne of Naples, whom Piero had known a number of years before when he was sent to Naples as Lorenzo's ambassador. He had recently learned how much power and wealth the Court of Naples had amassed and he fully intended to find a means to attach himself to it.

Alfonso was twenty eight. He had been married for five years and already had three children. He had a reputation of being refined but determined to have whatever he wanted. Simonetta remembers thinking that Piero was trying to position her to be something Alfonso wanted very badly. She can still see his regal figure as he stood before her in the midst of the merriment.

How amusing. Alfonso is dressed in the most elaborate uniform, even more grandiose than is customary for his position and especially for the skilled soldier he is reputed to be. I cannot help noticing that he is quite impressive and most handsome, just as Piero said. He bows to show his respect and then, without warning, searches among the folds of my dress to grab my hand. Without hesitating, almost as if he were leading a charge, he pulls me through the crowd that has gathered in the courtyard. His hand holds mine so firmly that I try to wrench it from him to escape the pain. I want to scream out.

I look around, hoping to see Lorenzo or Giuliano, even Piero, anyone who could stop this man from stealing me away from the protection of my family and especially from my friends.

Without a word he drags me up the stairs, through several rooms, even through the Hall of Justice where Maiano's work of covering the ceiling in pure gold is still in progress. Before I can utter a sound, I find myself on the loggia overlooking the city. I am breathless from the exertion.

Alfonso, still holding my hand, turns abruptly and falls to his knees. I am dumbfounded.

"I have heard of your beauty and comportment, but I can find no words to describe how radiant you are nor can I express how I am transported to realms I have never dreamed of by your presence. I adore you. I shall adore you for the rest of my life. I will never find anyone else to compare to you. You are the Venus of my dreams. The embodiment of all I have ever imagined the most perfect woman to be."

When Alfonso pauses to take a breath, I remove my hand

from his. I have never before encountered such effusive behavior. Trying not to show my surprise, and to be honest, my amusement at Alfonso's prodigious profession of love, I respond. I know exactly what to say. Many years of dealing with Piero have taught me the formula.

"And, I, Signore, have heard of your excellent qualities, of your bravery and cleverness in battle. Lorenzo holds you in great esteem. My father-in-law, whom you have known for many years, is your devotee. I consider myself honored to receive your declarations."

Alfonso, still on his knees, begins to grapple with my dress. As his hands advance further and further along the folds of the fabric and toward my waist, his intent becomes obvious.

In desperation and with some difficulty, I grab both his hands and pull with all my strength. As I am trying to force him to stand, I say as sweetly as I can, in a low voice. "I am greatly pleased by your attentions, Your Grace. But, Signore, I do not think now is the time nor here the place for us to engage in a realization of the passions you profess. Nor would I choose this time to express my respects for you in more than words."

I begin to back away from Alfonso, still holding his hands. This action forces Alfonso to rise to his feet.

"Please, Your Grace. Let us return to those who are waiting for us below. Lorenzo always notices when I am not present."

When Alfonso is fully upright, he is a changed man. He no longer seems the passionate suitor, but an ordinary man disappointed in the pursuit of his goal. Almost a boy, abashed by his own advances.

132

"You are right, Madonna. Now is neither the time nor the place. But you will remain forever in my heart as I have seen you tonight. I will always carry the vision of you as you are in this moment, a most remarkable portrait executed by The Great Artist."

Alfonso bows. "And now, my lady, I would be most grateful if you would precede me in returning to the courtyard. I will wait here a while to enjoy the view."

As I turn to go, happy to be returning to safety, I know Piero will not be pleased. I am sure he expected me to fulfill Alfonso's wishes and thus procure for him a new posting as Ambassador to the King of Naples.

Simonetta barely remembers finding her way back through the maize of rooms that Alfonso had recently propelled her through with such haste. She blushes recalling the speculations that circulated around Florence for the next several weeks regarding her encounter with His Majesty. She had felt ashamed even though she had done nothing except disappoint two men, each accustomed to having his own way.

Simonetta begins to cough. At the same time she is struggling to control her coughing, she feels a growing melancholy. And an inexplicable guilt. A sorrow for Alfonso. Why should one so enamored of another have none of that person's affection in return? Since her encounter with Alfonso, Piero has frequently brought her love letters and passionate poems from him, but she has never seen him again alone.

15

Although Simonetta is awake, her eyes are closed and she is reminiscing again.

28 January, 1475. The most important day of my life. The day of the great tournament Lorenzo gave to celebrate Giuliano's manhood. And Lorenzo chose my 22nd birthday as the date for the festivities. Even now I cannot imagine anything more perfect.

That morning, I awoke with such a feeling of exhilaration that I could hardly wait to hurl myself out of bed. Not a wise choice, for I was still warm from the quilts and the room was icy cold.

The dress I had designed for this occasion was the very essence of spring. Over its heavy white silk were scattered embroidered pink violets for faithfulness, yellow primroses for enduring love, and lilies of the valley for happiness. A gold band of embroidered laurel leaves, in Lorenzo's honor, encircled my breasts and continued, doubled, down the front of my skirt. Over the dress, I wore a cloak of finest French velvet in the pomegranate color I adore. It, too, was embroidered with spring flowers and in the center of each blossom was sewn a pearl which I had carefully selected from the jewelers. Dozens of pearls. But what I wore at my bosom was the greatest delight of all.

A few days before the tournament as we walked around the garden at Careggi, Giuli took a small gold coffer from the pocket of his cloak and placed it on my palm. He gently folded my hand over it with a sheepish grin, and asked me to open it. The treasure that was inside is the most beautiful gift I have ever received. A brooch of perfectly wrought gold with six gigantic pearls representing the Medici coat of arms. In the center is my birthstone which must be the largest garnet in existence. The total effect is magnificent. Best of all, Giuliano had designed and ordered it as a token of his love.

Consi helped me pin the brooch right in the center of my breasts. I have never felt nor, as I remember, ever looked more elegant and desirable. I was Venus, I was Flora, I was truly Primavera. And I was to be the official Queen of the Tournament, an exquisite jewel in my own ornate box.

That day as Giuliano rode into the arena at Santa Croce as the head of the grand procession, the banner created by Lorenzo to honor me waved out behind him. The silver helmet and armor detailed with the head of Medusa designed by Verrocchio glinted in the sun. I could not help but think of how he had changed since the day I had first seen him at Lorenzo's tournament six years before. Then he was a mere boy. On this day he was a full grown man of almost twenty-two, tall and straight and handsome! All of Florence cheered him. Dignitaries from all over Italy and beyond to France and Spain saw his grandeur. Despite my efforts to the contrary, I was full of pride.

I shall never forget that spectacle. Giuli was followed by Lorenzo and behind him fifty of the most important young noblemen of Florence, each arrayed in extravagant livery, their armament glittering in the sun and the banners proclaiming their loves waving out behind them. The workshops had been busy for weeks turning out these elaborate creations. The hands of that young artist from Vinci, Leonardo, must be still aching from constantly holding a pen.

The banner Giuli carried was designed by Sandro and made of Alexandrian silk taffeta with threads of gold and silver. The fabric was so fine Sandro was required to use the most delicate brush for painting on it. There, I am portrayed as Venus, a soft and shimmering muse given to love with Cupid at my head. The image is so ethereal that only someone as talented as Sandro could have executed it.

Sandro. My dear little Botticelli. Although he is my senior by nine years and much, much larger in size, he is still my little Botticelli. When Lorenzo asked him to draw me with the azure felt boots of Minerva and with a gold plated armor under my dress, Sandro accused him of trying to make me the symbol of a conquering goddess as well as a fragile beauty. He declared Lorenzo was attempting to find perfection in one woman just as the inscription he had chosen for the banner indicated. La Sans Par. *The one without equal. Since then I have often thought I should try harder to be the embodiment of that motto, both the virtuous woman and a conquering goddess. Ah, what a confusion of ideals these myths reflect.*

Which reminds me of Angelo Poliziano whom Lorenzo

calls his "Poet of the Republic." Angelo is still working on his epic chivalric poem to describe Giuliano's tournament and my part in Giuli's life. I enjoy envisioning myself as Angelo does, a nymph who captivates every courtier's heart and especially the one whom he calls Julio. However, I am not sure Angelo will ever finish his account. Book I is already 125 stanzas long, and he has just begun writing Book II. I am certain I will appear in the last verses as a decrepit old lady. Oh, dear me.

Angelo never tires of finding some excuse for praising Giuliano, either in his books or to his friends. He describes Giuli tall and muscular, a master at riding, throwing, jumping and wrestling. He never forgets to mention Giuli's ravenous taste for hunting. He brags continually that all the noble women in Florence lust after Giuliano's body and every wench has tried the most nefarious tactics to obtain that same body for herself. I have never stopped being jealous when Angelo talks so. The blood rises to my face at the thought of any other woman even looking at Giuli.

Despite Angelo's innuendos to the contrary, I do still believe Giuli thinks solely of me. Loves only me. Poliziano says Giuli thinks of me as his "Ideal of Spiritual and Physical Beauty" through which he can attain a union with perfection. Oh, my. So like Angelo to express our love in Platonic ideals. May God have mercy. What a deception, this Neo-Platonic dream of a love which is unattainable and therefore much more desirable and sacred.

What I crave is a physical love, sensual and carnal. Not some mythological ideal. I long only for someone who will try to know me as I truly am. Someone who will devote himself to our mutual pleasure. Someone like Giuliano.

Giuli whispers over and over how he wants me to be his "Ideal" and love me from afar. Then he contradicts himself without hesitation and tells me that he desires me well beyond the strongest attraction he has ever felt for any other woman. Desires me with an appetite which by far surpasses any other he has ever known.

Not so very Platonic, I would say.

That day at tournament when Giuli stopped before me, bowed, offered me the banner and raised his eyes to mine, my very core was molten. I can feel the heat even now.

I want to bury myself under the quilts forever, experiencing the sheer delight of those moments.

Before Simonetta can command her body to move, she is distracted by a noise on the stairs. She pulls herself up a bit and tries to look alert. Not even Consi must know that she has been reliving Giuliano's tournament day again. Certainly Consi would chide her as always for living too much in the past.

"My lady, my lady." Consolata practically screams as she comes bursting into the room without knocking.

"I have some exciting news for you. Sandro is coming this afternoon to spend some time with you. Your little Botticelli. Your little barrel. He has just returned from the villa at Cafaggiolo and has sent his man round this morning to ask if you are well enough to receive him. Piero thought that he might visit just after the mid-day meal and before the doctors arrive this afternoon."

"I am so excited, Consi. I cannot wait to see my little barrel again."

"Come now. We must prepare you for this day. You must look your most captivating, in one of your best dresses and with your hair coiffed to hold strings of little pearls. I will weave them into the tiny braids that Sandro seems to love to sketch. Oh, you will look so beautiful that your dear devoted Botticelli will never suspect that you have not been as strong as usual. Then perhaps even you will be convinced of your imminent recovery.

"Come. We have much to do and little time to do it all. I'll run and get a warm basin of lavender water for you. Then I'll bring in rosemary to freshen the room and some of those beautiful little violets for the vase on your table. I will have you and this stale old room looking fit for an occasion of state. You'll see. And when the doctors come later, they will be amazed at your recovery."

As soon as Consolata leaves the room, Simonetta practically flings herself out of bed, her anticipation of seeing Sandro is so great.

16

When the door opens a crack, Simonetta is startled from her reverie at the writing desk where she is beginning a letter to Giuliano. As she turns toward the noise, the door opens even more to reveal a face peering in at her. She rises to go to the door just as Sandro Botticelli flings it open and comes bounding into the room toward her. He is followed by Consolata and Caterina. All his youthful exuberance is still evident in his loping stride and his rosy face set off by that curly red hair which remains untamed and flamboyant.

"What's this I hear about you being ill? You look as beautiful and healthy as ever. I will never believe those gossips again!"

"Oh, Sandro. Let me look at you."

Simonetta holds out her arms as if to grab him by the shoulders, but instead she pulls him to her and gives him a strong embrace. His body feels reassuring and forceful, but she releases him quickly. Caterina is in the room and even though she is like a mother to Sandro and Sandro almost like a brother to herself, too much hesitation might make her mother-in-law suspicious that there is more than a sisterly love arising in Simonetta.

"My dear, dear friend," Simonetta begins. "I am so glad to see you. You can never know how glad. I have missed you so. You are that magnanimous spirit that makes my heart glad whenever you are near."

Botticelli replies. "And you exude that unparalleled beauty that makes all my study and all my painting worthwhile. For Florence you are the idealization of beauty, but for me, your face is the face I will always see as that of every Venus, every Madonna, every beautiful woman I paint. Your face in all its astonishing perfection and all its various moods."

Simonetta reddens. It has been a long time since she has been around such flattery.

Sandro doesn't notice, but continues. "Maybe I should promise you right this moment that I will never again paint another woman's face. No young, beautiful woman that I portray will have a face other than yours. I kneel before you, my dear Simonetta, my only love, my ideal of earthly and heavenly beauty."

Sandro drops to his knees, takes Simonetta's hand and pretends to kiss it.

"Now what do you think of that? Will you accept me as your admirer, a devotee forever? Will you allow me to worship all that you are; intellect, beauty, friend. Will you let me remain at your feet adoring you for my lifetime and after, be buried there in death?"

Simonetta removes her hand from Sandro's and laughs.

"Stop it, Sandro. Stand up. You are such a tease. And you are making me blush. Caterina must think you most forward. And here I am, just a child compared to your advanced years. You know I am barely 23 and you have already passed your 31st birthday. I have been occupying my time lately with sketching designs for a cane that will help you in your old age."

Sandro rises from his knees and wobbles about a bit pretending he is already in need of a cane, which makes Simonetta laugh even harder.

All conversation is interrupted as Consolata returns with an extra chair, so that the three can sit down and have some refreshments. Caterina takes the chair closest to the door. She has no intention of spending her afternoon listening to this silly chatter, but she plans to stay long enough to take a sip of the Vin Santo wine that Consolata will be bringing.

Simonetta turns to Sandro and asks, "Are you close to finishing your latest project? I have been telling Consolata that I am anxious to go again to Santa Maria Novella and see what progress you have made on the *Adoration of the Magi*. Consi proclaims it most incredible. She says that the colors are brilliant and the composition is innovative and intriguing. That the portraits are so well executed that I would know the faces of everyone in the painting."

Caterina, who has not uttered a word since she arrived, becomes suddenly animated and sits up on the edge of her chair. "You would be so pleased, Simonetta. Sandro has painted the Medicis as only he can do. Cosimo is kneeling at the feet of the Madonna who is presenting the Christ child to him. He looks so elegant and wise, just as we all remember him."

Caterina hesitates a moment, then she starts to grin.

"But, shame on you, Sandro. It would seem you have inverted the personalities of Lorenzo and Giuliano. Giuli looks staid and regal in his black coat. And Lorenzo looks every bit the mischievous boy. Is this another of the jokes you love to play? Who will believe that those two are as you have painted them? Lorenzo's face on Giuliano's body and vice versa. I am glad it is not our family paying you a fortune for this diversion of yours."

"And did you notice, my dear Madonna, how I painted Piero de' Medici and Giovanni, his brother? I guess I am quite an expert now at painting dead Medici.

"Of course I don't mean to be impertinent, Madonna. Really. I want the painting to be timeless. As a matter of fact, I was trying to pay homage to the most influential men of the Accademia and to those leaders in positions of power the Medici have supported through these last few years. And, of course, with no ulterior motive, you understand. All this portraiture has nothing to do with increasing my commissions. Do you really think, Madonna Catrina, I painted Giuliano as too pretentious?'

"You will have to ask him that question. But you mustn't take me too seriously, Sandro. You know I have always loved to tease you. Although, I must say, you do look unforgivably serious in that painting as you stare at the viewers with your self-assured visage. Looking upon that face, I would not dream of arguing with you at all."

Consolata enters and places a tray on the writing table. It holds intricately etched gold-edged Venetian wine glasses, a matching carafe with wine, and a silver plate of figs and cantucci, Simonetta's favorite type of biscotti. She then brings a small serving table from outside the door, spreads an embroidered linen cloth on it and places it in the center of the chairs where everyone is seated at the foot of Simonetta's bed. Next she transfers the items from the tray to the serving table.

Consolata picks up the carafe and asks, "Would you care for wine, Madonna Caterina? Signor Botticelli?

Caterina turns to her guest. "Sandro, try a bit of this Vin Santo di San Gimignano. It has been aged eight years and is the best vin santo one can buy at the moment. I will join you. It is one of my favorites. Will you take some too, Simonetta?"

"Not just now, thank you, Madonna. I am much more interested in learning more about what other work Sandro is doing. Are you still working on the interior of Il Duomo with your artist friends? The rumor is that instead you have started painting on your own again and you have just finished a painting of your brother, Antonio. He is showing off the medal he has just cast in gold, that of Cosimo the Elder. I would love to see that painting. Are you hiding it in your workshop, Sandro?"

Caterina smiles at Simonetta's insistence on hearing more about her friend's work. She takes a sip of her wine, and then sits forward again, putting a nearly full glass on the table.

"My dears, please accept my apologies, but I must leave you now. Piero has left me with a list of tasks to complete for him. He still counts on me to do his accounting and to write most of his letters. It is as if I have nothing to do other than his work. My own lists of household chores and acquisitions go begging.

"One last word, Sandro. Giorgio Antonio... I'm sure you must remember Piero's brother... who respects your work as we all do, is talking of having you paint a companion piece to Ghirlandaio's *St. Jerome* for our Vespucci chapel in Ognissanti. I have encouraged him to do so. He is considering a portrait of St. Augustine, since he is a saint so respected by our Umiliati brothers and so venerated by all Florence as the meditative scholar. A very representative personage for the Vespuccis, wouldn't you say?"

Caterina smiles for the first time.

"If I may venture a guess, I would say Antonio wants you to make your *Saint Augustine* even more august than Ghirlandaio's *Jerome*. A little competition is always a good thing. And I am confident you wouldn't mind trying your skills against Domenico's. May the best man win.

"All of Florence is praising your talent right now. *The Adoration* has brought you much admiration from all of us. No wonder we have had to give you up so often to other cities so that they can share in some of our good fortune of having you as a native son."

"As always, you flatter me too much, my sweet Madonna."

"Please give my regards to your parents. Our home is always open to you. God go with you."

As Caterina rises, Botticelli rises also and gives a slight bow.

"Goodbye, my dearest Madonna. I do not know how I would have survived without your continued support through all these years. I thank you especially for all the delicious fruits and jams and cheeses you have sent round to my studio in these recent months. Were it not for your attentions, I may well have starved. My mother practically ignores my existence these days, so I am more than ever justified in regarding you as a second mother, for that you have been to me since our family has moved next door on Via del Porcellana. Please give all of my best regards to the rest of the family. And especially to Madonna Nonna. May God be with you all."

Reluctantly, Caterina turns toward the door to take her leave. She has always delighted in Sandro's high spirits and frequently catches herself wishing her own son were more like him.

Once the door has closed behind her mother-in-law,

Simonetta leans a little closer to Sandro and puts her hand over his on the table.

"Dear, dear Sandro, now that I have you all to myself, we can talk of more personal things, like the question that has been haunting me for years. And which you refuse to answer. Maybe this time you will satisfy my curiosity. How is it you are still making your reputation as "Botticelli?" Does your father not reproach you that you have not retained the family name? Do you not think Alessandro di Mariano di Vanni Filipepi is a more auspicious name than "little barrel." Please convince me this name did not come because you drink too much. Or because you are built so strong as to resemble a barrel."

Simonetta has often teased him about his name and Sandro has no intention of responding to her questions despite her most recent plea. He just gives a little smile.

Simonetta continues.

"Since you have never given me a satisfactory answer to this question, I will attempt to elicit a response to an even more important concern of mine. I need to know if you have been following the advice of Cennini? I'm sure you are acquainted with what he says in his artist's handbook, *Il Libro dell'Arte*. "One must avoid indulging too much in the company of women or one's hands will shake more than leaves in the wind." Have you been wise, Sandro? Have you been following Cennini's dictates? May I assume your hands have not been shaking but have been appropriately occupied with your paintings now that Lorenzo and Giuliano are in

Pisa and their constant temptations with them."

Sandro smiles again, but continues to say nothing.

"Oh, how I have missed you these last weeks and months when you have been so busy. It seems like forever since we have all been together at Careggi."

Sandro lets Simonetta continue. He is intently studying her face.

"I have not returned since we were all there for the November banquet celebrating Plato's birthday. Do you remember how we spent the hours that evening discussing the immortality of the soul? How each of us vowed we would give up carnal pursuits for a divine and God-like beauty?

"When you conceive a painting, do you consider all these ideals we have discussed or do you think strictly of the line and composition? Of trying to capture and render the reality of the beauty you see with your own eyes."

Finally Sandro speaks.

"My dear Simonetta, you have become much too serious in these last few months. This preoccupation with the soul and the nature of beauty is all well and good for the discussions at Careggi, but for me, when I am being the artist, I think first of beauty, earthy and earthly. In the outward presentation of the person, I try to portray the face and body as close to reality as I can. But it is the hidden reality that each person carries within, often a torment unrecognized even by himself, that fascinates me. Therefore I must admit I do also really try to reflect the soul in the face of each person I paint. I believe the soul and the body are inexorably intertwined.

"But see here, young lady. You have made me become much too serious as well and it does not become me to be serious. Let's talk of you. Are you feeling stronger now that spring has come and you can open your window and dream of walking the hills once more?"

Simonetta smiles at Sandro's concern.

"Each day, I do feel stronger. And I do dream of walking the hills. But most of all, I dream of being at Careggi. Feeling the fresh mountain air, walking the gardens or sitting in the Great Hall with the doors open to the loggia overlooking the valley. Don't you think Cosimo would be proud of the way his grandsons have carried out his dream of Careggi becoming a center of learning and art? The true Neo-Platonic Society.

Sandro smiles at Simonetta's comment.

"I, too, am anxious to be back there. Soon we will all be reunited."

Shifting a little in his chair which is much too delicate for his large frame, Sandro attempts to change the subject.

"What do you think of the latest of Poliziano's *Stanze* on Giuliano's tournament? I am flattered he has based much of the story on the mythology and design I used in the banner I made for Giuliano."

Simonetta winces at the thought of the banner.

"That banner is my most precious possession.

149

Giuliano has never stopped begging me to let him take it to Via Largo to hang over his bed. He says over and over again, 'I shall die if I cannot see your beauty the last second before I sleep and when I first open my eyes each morning.' Do you hear the way he talks to me? How can I help but think seriously of letting him take it to Via Largo on the very first day he returns to me."

Sandro smiles.

"Perhaps I will make a new one just for you. It will show you as you are now, with your more fragile beauty and all the wisdom you have gained over the past year. But you have reminded me to ask when you have last heard from Giuliano. Will he be coming home soon?"

"I haven't heard from Giuliano in over a week, but Madonna Lucrezia wrote only two days ago to say that Giuliano left Pisa as soon as he heard of my illness. He is on his way here now.

"Oh, dear Sandro, I have missed him so. Am I terribly selfish to be glad he did not receive the letter from Piero telling Lorenzo that I am better? I feel I cannot contain myself until he arrives. He should be here in two days if he is not delayed by the spring rains."

"Well then," Sandro smiles, "it will not be long now. Happily there is little left for you to do in the next few days except to get ready to receive Giuliano and prepare to resume your quite satisfying life."

Sandro rises from his chair.

"My dear Simonetta, I regret that 1 need to take

150

my leave now. I must not let the oils dry on the portrait of Madonna Esmeralda I am painting for Signor Bandinilli. He would not be happy to receive a corrected canvas. He is knowledgeable enough to know immediately where there is an over painting. Pity. Besides, the doctors will be appearing any moment and you must have time to rest a little and compose yourself."

"Two doctors. One small patient. Where is the symmetry?" Simonetta replies.

Sandro stoops to place a kiss on her forehead.

"Dear Simonetta, you should consider yourself a fortunate woman. I am leaving now and I have spared you from even the most gentle of my practical jokes. You are much too beautiful for practical jokes."

Sandro Botticelli is obviously flustered when he continues. "However, I do not joke when I say your face haunts me whenever I sit down to paint. It appears in my dreams. I sometimes imagine what a happy man I would be now if I had been the husband accompanying you on your wedding journey. Alas, my dear, I am sure you would never have been able to stand the smell of oil and turpentine for all these years. Let alone the stink I cause in any other way I can contrive."

When Simonetta looks up at her friend to laugh at his teasing, her movement is interrupted by a cough.

Simonetta rises carefully and falteringly, then moves toward Sandro. She lays her right hand on his shoulder and stretches upward toward him. She gives him a firm kiss on the cheek and settles down off her tiptoes.

"Sandro, you always cheer me. How have I managed your being away for so long? You, my adopted brother, who makes me grateful for all my brothers, even the ones lost to me. Do come again soon, dearest Sandro."

Consolata moves forward from the shadows by the door.

"I will walk with you to the courtyard," she offers.

"Please don't disappoint me, Sandro. Come soon. I am lonely here in this room."

"I give you my solemn promise I will return within the week. And I will bring with me a charcoal sketch of you as I see you in my dreams. Venus arriving at Portovenere, the Cinque Terre behind you."

17

Simonetta returns to her bed. Even before she can drift into a light sleep, Giuliano is with her again. She is reliving the last time she was with him at Careggi. They are standing in the garden, where the lemon trees are just beginning to bud. Giuliano is staring into her eyes.

I have never seen Giuli so serious. He is searching my eyes as though he wishes to see into the deepest part of me. Abruptly, he lowers his eyes from mine and grabs my hand. Yes, grabs, as if he were angry or somehow compelled by something outside himself. Surprised by his force and his haste, I resist as he pulls me forward, never looking back. He is practically dragging me through the garden. His determination is so strong that I almost cry out.

The panic I feel is not lessening. Is he angry with me? Have I done something to displease him? Could he have heard of the letter I received from Alfonso only a few days ago?

As we pass through the gate at the foot of the garden path and gain the open land, Giuliano eases his grasp a bit so my wrist is no longer aching. I stop pulling back just a little. Although I am still stumbling along behind him, I am no longer at that awkward angle when every step feels like a threatened fall.

I know better than to ask Giuli where he is taking me. I know better than to utter any small sound that would make him turn back toward me and break the spell that has come over him. Although he is still moving quickly, he has eased in his posture and his grip enough that I feel as if he has eased in his mind as well.

Perhaps Giuli is just overcome with desire. Perhaps he is so anxious to take me in his arms and kiss me that he can have no other thought than to spirit me away for some hidden tryst. My own eagerness is growing.

The slope of the land gentles a bit as we approach the rows of grape vines that angle out below us on the hillside. The spring sun has warmed the earth so that I can feel it through my slippers which are made for walking on limestone floors and not over the clods of dirt.

I am certain I know where we are going. Well beyond the view of the villa. Even out of sight of the loggia which juts out at the southwest end of it. To a small glade where oaks and elms grow in great profusion, providing shade, a coolness that seems almost damp on such a day. Not surprisingly, a rill runs through it. Giuliano and I have gone there often to escape the constant surveillance of even the most accepting of our friends.

Many of our friends are intrigued by our devotion to one another. More accurately stated, they are envious. They wish to understand and perhaps to emulate us as they search for some mythic ideal that is all beauty and purity and pretense. Pomp and circumstance, not boiling blood and sweating passion.

154

Without even the slightest pause to look back at me, Giuliano marches down the slope as if he were about to attack an enemy. I follow with a mixture of curiosity and anticipation. Even a little fear. I have never seen Giuliano so intent, so steeled, as if a bit of fiendishness has managed to slip into his affable personality.

As we reach the end of the vineyard, my heart is pounding so loudly, surely Giuli must hear it. Skirting around the olive trees reportedly planted by the Romans during their conquest, I imagine for a second I am seeing fully armored shadows lurking behind each tree. Am I going mad? Unlike most days in the past, I barely notice the exotic beauty of their truncated limbs.

Abruptly I am brought back to reality when I stub the big toe of my right foot on a rather large protruding root. After a startling re-entry into the real world, I immerse myself in the sensitivities of my own body and its every acute sensation. I hardly notice how my limbs are shaking with the exertion of the descent.

At the foot of the vineyard, the land levels out before it plunges into the little grove. Here, Giuliano stops suddenly and turns to face me. He does not let go of my hand. The expression on his face is unfathomable. A mixture of hope and questioning. A demeanor such as I have never seen on his face before. My eyes search his, as I too become very aware of how solemn this outing has become. His severe, almost painful, examination of my face disquiets me.

Without a word, he turns again to the little path we have worn in the forest floor with our frequent visits. Still holding my hand, he walks slowly forward.

When we reach the center of the small stand of trees, Giuli releases my hand and turns toward me. He places his right hand under my chin and lifts my face to look into his again. He is not smiling, but the expression in his eyes, which are looking directly into mine, is gentle.

Without saying a word, he drops his hand to my waist and pulls me toward him. I do not resist. The urgency I sense in his body makes my own respond fervently. As I wrap my arms around him, my body fuses with his. I move my hands to the center of his back and hold him as tightly against me as my strength permits.

Everything I have ever known, ever experienced, ever dreamt converges in this transcendent moment. Giuli and I are one, standing in the middle of this wild garden, the sunlight filtering through the trees overhead and the rest of the world at bay. One body. One soul.

18

With a newly written letter to Lorenzo in his hand, Piero stands quietly outside Simonetta's door. He has tried to ascend the stairs so stealthily that she will not be aware he is coming. Once he nears her door, his courage fails him. He had planned to make her aware that those whom she loves have deserted her and have left him alone in his attempt to care for her. He wonders how he was able to negotiate for Lorenzo in foreign courts and financial institutions, while here in his own home he feels cowed and inadequate before one vulnerable young woman.

Brusquely he stuffs the letter, so carefully folded, into his vest pocket and taps quietly on the door. He is not sure if the knock is loud enough to be heard because, in truth, he is hoping Simonetta will not answer nor bid him come in. How like a thirteen year old boy he feels, standing at her door, shaking from fear about how he will appear and what he will say to her once he is in her presence. But, he reminds himself, he has not visited in almost a week.

Appearances dictate that he should at least inquire after her health and wish her a good day.

Yes, that is what he will do. Not a word about the doctors' squabbles or about their observations that she is no better; in fact, perhaps worse. Not a word about all the friends and family who have not yet responded to his letters about her illness.

No sound is coming from the room. A reprieve, he thinks to himself as he turns to go back to his study. Just then he sees that Consolata is coming up the steps.

"I will go in and wake her, Signore. She has probably fallen into another sleep. She will be quite happy to see you. Please wait so I can be sure she is prepared to receive you."

Being told by a servant to wait outside the door of his daughter-in-law's room is infuriating to him. He has been a man of such importance that he has rarely been told to wait even by lords and kings. He bristles. Of late, he has been failing in his relationship with Lorenzo. It has been months since he has been sent on an important mission.

"Please give Simonetta my regards," he responds quickly. "I will return at another time when she is perhaps more disposed to receive me. I have my own affairs to attend to now."

And with those abrupt words, he turns and starts toward the stairs.

For a moment, Consolata is so stunned she stares after him. However, Consolata seldom needs more than an instant to recover herself, no matter the occasion. She turns and opens the door. Tiptoeing in, she observes Simonetta lying on her bed with an enraptured expression on her face. Consolata's countenance changes from that of a devoted servant looking into her mistress's sleeping face into the epitome of sorrow.

Slowly Simonetta opens her eyes. How long she and Giuli have stood entwined without the least movement or sound, she does not know. Time has disappeared: other people, other places, even the small jewel-like woodlet around them have all disappeared.

She does not want to leave the comfort she feels envisioning herself with Giuliano on the last day they were together. She is exactly where she wants to be and would happily let her dream world hold her forever.

Consolata does not say a word, but arranges the freshly pressed linen shifts in the cassone and opens the shutters a bit wider. Then she stands at the foot of the window and waits for her mistress to show some signs of acknowledging her presence so she can go on with her duties.

"How long have you been here, Consi?"

"Only a few minutes, my lady. I have just come up to see if you need anything. I was taken aback to find Signor Vespucci at your door. I believe he had already knocked, but once I told him you might be sleeping, he said to give you his regards and wish you a good day.

"You had such a lovely smile on your face when I came in, you must have been dreaming."

"I was dreaming. Only I wish it were not a dream but a reality. Giuliano was with me. We were walking through the gardens at Careggi. The everyday world disappeared as we stood on the edge of the garden overlooking the springtime valley, its delicate golden buds covering all the hills. And the two of us stood there, loving each other as if we were immortal and were surveying a world without fear or strife."

"There is no wonder you did not want to wake up, my lady. Were it not a sin to covet, I would envy you your dream."

"Soon I will not be dreaming. Consi. Giuliano will be with me and I will not need to dream. When he is near, the intrusive world disappears. There might as well be a choir of angels singing us into heaven, because when I am near him, I know nothing of this earth."

"Come, my lady," Consi warns. "If you are not careful, you will certainly be dreaming again and I will have to abandon my duties for fear of disturbing your reveries."

"Has the courier been here yet this afternoon? I would be elated to receive a letter from Giuliano letting me know of his progress. He must be almost here. I can feel his presence, but I will be so grateful when I can feel his body as well. Surely some of his great strength will pass to me. Infuse me with the energy I have been lacking."

Consolata tries to hide her concern.

"I will go and check for the courier. I am sure he will pass today because Piero was writing letters while Biattina arranged his studio this morning. We servants are not supposed to notice or talk about such things, but how else can one keep up with what is happening in the household, my lady, if we who want to please you do not tattle?"

"As far as I am concerned, you and Biattina may take note and tattle about any and all the goings on you can manage to discover. However, to please me, you must tell me every morsel of gossip you can gather. But I think I hear the courier just now riding out. Please hurry to see if Giuli has sent any word."

As Consolata leaves the room, she is practically tripping over herself in her haste to get to Piero's study to inquire if there is indeed a letter for Simonetta. She flies down the stairs, taking them two at a time, but her speed in running back up the stairs is almost doubled. She has in her hand a letter that will surely make her mistress happy.

Quietly she opens the door, which she has left unlatched so she can enter without disturbing Simonetta. Her caution is unnecessary. Simonetta is sitting up in bed. In her anticipation she has smoothed the covers and plumped the pillows herself. Her face has taken on a pinkish glow and she is smiling one of her old smiles. The same smile that conquered all of Florence.

Consolata realizes she too is smiling to see her mistress happy and looking well. If only Giuliano were already here. After a few glances exchanged with him, Simonetta would surely recover completely.

"You have guessed it, my lady. Here is the letter you

have been hoping for. Now, what will you pay me for it?" Consi holds the letter high above her head and continues. "I have always admired that banner Botticelli made for Giuliano's tournament. I have also had my eye on the old silver mirror from home that you keep hidden in your cassone. I could use that ram's bristle brush with the horn handle. Or, maybe…"

"Stop, Consolata. You are such a tease. And I have already had to put up with Sandro this afternoon. Quick, quick. Give the letter to me and I will reward you by reading it out loud."

"Goodness, my lady. That is not such a grand offer. You are the one who is rewarded by what Signor Giuliano writes, not I."

"Ah, yes, Consi. But I know you well enough to know that you delight in every little tidbit you can gather about us "two lovebirds" as you call us. I forbid you to breathe a word of what Giuliano has written to anyone else. Not even to Biattina."

"Of course, my lady. I promise. Now please, my lady, read."

19

My dearest, my beloved Simonetta,

Would that I were already there to tell you myself of our progress, but I am close by and can hardly take a breath without nearly fainting in the anticipation of seeing you and holding you again. How long the way from Pisa has been on my return!

Our party stopped at Empoli last night to refresh the horses as well as ourselves. Often we have been able to make the trip from Pisa to Florence in only two days, but the spring rains have made the roads so muddy we barely cover twenty kilometers in a day. And even then, we are all exhausted from the struggle through the mire.

Do not despair. If I can prod our group along, I am hoping to arrive in Florence tomorrow evening, very late. Or at the latest, the evening of the 24th. I will send round word as soon as I arrive and I will come immediately to see you, should you like. Lorenzo has sent word by his courier that the doctors say you are much improved, so I shall not hesitate to visit you whenever and for as long as you wish. I beg you to receive me as soon as possible upon hearing of my return. I am without guile in my pursuit of our reunion.

I apologize that this letter is so short, but we are all very weary. The provisions are few here in this modest hostel, and we arose early this morning to try to make Florence before dark tomorrow night. If God so wishes, we will meet no later than the 25th. And I am praying every minute that I will find you nearly recovered so we can be together again at Careggi in the coming weeks.

I can dream of nothing but the rapture I felt when the two of us were last together. Every night I fall asleep reliving those moments, dreaming of being with you again, of …. But I will hold in check my fantasies and simply pray that soon spring sunlight, sweet perfumed air and my presence will bring about a return of the rosy color to your dear cheeks.

I cannot wait to kiss those cheeks. All day as I ride, I evoke your image. I barely notice the country or streams through which we travel. I think only of you. Forever and beyond death, I am your devoted servant, your loyal friend, and your most ardent admirer. My life without you would no longer be a life worth living.

I send you my undying love,
Your most humble servant,
Giuliano de' Medici
Written from Empoli,
22 April 1476

Simonetta closes her eyes. An angelic smile appears on her lips. While Consolata waits patiently beside her, Simonetta slowly lowers the letter, as if she were under a spell. After a few minutes, she suddenly sits upright and begins dictating to Consolata.

164

"Quick, Consi, go to the cassone and take out my green velvet dress. It must be wrinkled and musky by now. You must take it to the courtyard and let it breathe the air of spring. Stuff the sleeves with the potpourri from last winter and place a large bouquet of dried lavender in the bodice. Never will it have had such an auspicious day as the day I wear it for Giuliano's return.

"Look, Consi. Already the color is coming back into my cheeks. He will be here in only one or two days. There is so much to do.

"You must fetch the hairdresser for early tomorrow morning. And have Arturo go gather rosemary from the hills of Fiesole. Bouquets of it. Have him check the spot just below the cliffs to see if the lavender is in bloom. And check my powders to be sure everything is in order. If not, you will need to run round to the apothecary's no later than tomorrow morning before I wake.

"And my shoes. I will wear my velvet slippers, but they must be spotless. And do not forget the brooch that Giuliano gave me for my birthday last year, the one with the gigantic garnet and the extraordinary pearls.

"Or perhaps should I wear the cameo Giuli gave me during our first year together, the one that has Apollo and Minerva carved into the agate. We both love that one. I have often teased Giuliano that he is bound by my love as Apollo was by Minerva. What a lovely story. Not only is that brooch full of meaning for both of us, but it really goes better with my dress.

"Of course, the newer brooch means even more to me because Giuliano designed it himself. I ..."

"Madonna, Madonna. Slow down. I will never remember all of these instructions if they come tumbling out of your mouth in such a rush. Here, now, let's start with the dress. I will pull it from its place in the cassone and after it has aired, you can look at it with each brooch and make this important decision about which one you prefer.

"And will you be wearing the pearls in your hair? I believe Piero has taken them to his study for safekeeping."

"Of course, for safe keeping. And possibly to show off to visitors. He is so proud of those pearls. He has always wanted my portrait painted with them in my hair. I am sure I would have to be drawn in three quarter profile to show them off to advantage. Piero often talks of a young goldsmith who is only 15, but has already shown great promise as a portrait painter. I believe his name is Cosimo.

"Can you imagine? I am to be used as a model to show off Piero's good taste. I'm not sure that idea would surprise anyone. He would probably hang it in his study just to brag whenever someone came to visit.

"Oh, do forgive me, Consolata. I have become more acerbic as I have grown weaker. I have promised myself I will think only positive thoughts. I will smile every moment of the day and night in anticipation of Giuliano's return and our first trip together to Careggi."

"After Lorenzo is back in Florence, I will visit him at Via Largo. We can all go and sit in the sunshine of the lemonaria, enjoying the scent of the lemon blossoms and feeling the warmth of the spring sun on our shoulders. What a delicious dream. For me, that garden is the loveliest spot in the palazzo.

"Of course, I should be reprimanded for not naming Gozzoli's chapel as the most beautiful. But then, considering that Donatello's *David* is in the courtyard, maybe... How is one to choose? And the miracle is that I do not have to choose one or the other. The truth is that I will be happy simply to be with Lorenzo and to have Giuliano by my side. I feel like running up those grand stairs to the chapel and down again for sheer joy."

"Madonna, calm yourself. You will be exhausted from just imagining all this activity. Rest a little. I will go and begin our preparations for Giuliano's arrival."

Simonetta cannot stop the words from tumbling out of her mouth.

"Oh, Consi, I can hardly wait to join the Accademia again, even though at this time of year they have not yet gone to Careggi. They will go there soon and I will be able to visit Lucrezia in her sanctuary off of the Loggia. It is a small room, but the sun flows in there so beautifully about mid-day this time of year. How many pleasant lunches we have taken right outside of her room under the loggia.

"And when I get to Careggi, I will certainly run down the hill to visit Maestro Ficino in his cottage and sit with him for a few hours, watching him work on his translations and listening to his ever-ready wisdom.

"And then back up the hill to joke with Poliziano. Will he never finish his poem on Giuliano's joust? He would much rather create his bawdy rhymes at the tavern and make the company laugh. Or impress the Accademia with his knowledge of mythology.

"Oh, how I have missed everyone!"

"My lady. My lady. You must rest. You will begin coughing again and then you will need more medicine. Please be wise. Rest, for later the doctors will be visiting. You will need your strength."

"Can you not see, Consi? I cannot rest. My imaginings have taken over my body and my body is ready to take up life again. I am ready to dance and sing and kiss my love. I am ready for what life has in store for me. Do not insist that I refrain from living again, at least from my bed this afternoon. Oh, happy day!

"You go now, Consi. I will lie back, but I do not promise to rest. I promise only to dream. Such beautiful dreams."

Consolata gives Simonetta a kiss on the forehead. Her mistress these days has become more and more like her child.

Already Simonetta's eyes are closed again and she has fallen into another sleep.

Although she is only two years older than Simonetta,

Consolata still feels she has been a mother to her mistress ever since they left Piombino together, two naive young girls. Conci knows how well Catocchia loves her daughter, but she is puzzled that in all these years Catocchia has never come to visit. Especially now that Simonetta is so sick. She is sure Signor Piero must have written her of her daughter's illness. But, of course, not even the doctors had realized until the last few days just how serious Simonetta's affliction really is.

Consolata cannot stop the tears she feels welling up. She whispers to herself, "She is my child. My dear and only child. I must watch over her and make her well again. My child. I am responsible for her now."

Before she turns to go, Consolata touches Simonetta's hand and says, "Rest well, my child. May God attend you."

Part IV

26 April 1476

She is fair-skinned, unblemished white, and
white is her garment, though ornamented with
roses, flowers, and grass; the ringlets of her golden
hair descend on a forehead humbly proud.
The whole forest smiles about her, and, as it
may, lighten her cares; in her movement she is
regally mild, her glance alone could quiet a tempest.

44

From her eyes there flashes a honeyed calm in
which Cupid hides his torch; wherever she turns
those amorous eyes, the air about her becomes
serene. Her face, sweetly painted with privet and
roses, is filled with heavenly joy; every breeze is
hushed before her divine speech, and every little
bird sings out in its own language.

45

Beside her goes humble, gentle Chastity, who
turns the key to every locked heart; with her
goes Nobility with kindly appearance and imitates
her sweet graceful step. No base soul can
regard her face without first representing of it
faults; Love captures, wounds, and kills all those
hearts with whom she sweetly speaks or sweetly laughs.

Stanzas Begun for the Joust of the Magnificent Giuliano de Medici,
Book I by Angelo Poliziano

20

A shiver runs through me. The inside of the cathedral seems darker than usual, as if a storm were passing overhead.

I rise from my knees and sit back carefully. Balancing on the edge of the Vespucci pew, I try to spot Giuliano as he situates himself along the north wall beside the two other young men who have entered with him just moments before. I am surprised to see Giuli this Easter morning because Consolata reported earlier that he was ill and would not attend mass. I am even more surprised that his companions are Bernardo Bandini and Francesco de' Pazzi. Giuli once told me that he is unsure of their friendship and suspicious of the entire Pazzi family. Still Giuliano believes the peace must be maintained as one of his Medici sisters is married to a Pazzi.

"Ite, missa est," the priest pronounces. As the choir finishes singing, the eleven o'clock chimes ring and the priest begins the elevation of the Host. Everyone quiets, even the boisterous youths around Giuliano. Just at that moment close to Giuliano I see the glint of an upraised dagger, the same weapon I have seen so many

times before.

Then I see another blade. And another. I count four daggers before I scream. I scream so loudly everyone in the cathedral turns to look in my direction. My mother-in-law has a look of horror on her face. I break out in a cold sweat and begin shaking. I sense the air being forced from my lungs by each thrust downward of a honed point. I fling my hands over my breast to protect my heart.

And then I sit bolt upright.

Consolata is the first to arrive. But she is followed quickly by Biattina. Caterina, Bice and Ginevra, who have heard the screams as they were being served their breakfasts in the dining room, enter behind her.

Consolata rushes to the bed and pulls the covers up around Simonetta, holding her tight so she will stop shaking. Caterina stands at the foot of the bed, her hand grasping the bedpost. She looks as if she is witnessing a deathbed drama. Her daughters stand back in the shadows between the door and the window.

When Piero enters, they all curtsy slightly.

"What has happened here?" he asks of no one in particular.

When no one answers, Consolata says, almost in a whisper, "She has had another of her nightmares, Signore. I am sure. She is in a cold sweat and shaking all over. These terrors have been happening every night since Signori Lorenzo and Giuliano left for Pisa. They have been growing worse. Often she awakes, not only screaming but also coughing as if her lungs were ready to fly out of her body. I must hold her and talk to her of many things before she is calm enough to lie back down in bed."

Piero is not pleased.

"I sent for Maestro Stefano again, but he answered that there is nothing more he can do. Maestro Moyse says only God can manage her recovery now. However he promises me he will return today to administer to her as best he can. But solely because I have insisted he do so.

"I have also sent for Father Giuseppe. Simonetta has always favored him. Perhaps he can soothe her and rid her of these demons that haunt her dreams.

"She seems much weaker today. Has she taken anything to eat?" Piero shifts impatiently, as if this detail is almost more than he can manage.

"Not yet today, Signor Vespucci. It is her habit to take a little milk and perhaps one or two cantucci once she is fully awake and has regained her composure."

Caterina ventures. "She is very pale and much weaker today than when I came yesterday. I am more concerned than ever that she is losing her strength.

"Please do send for the priest right away, Husband. And I beg you to send a post to Maestro Moyse as well, telling him to leave everything and come straight away. I will stay with her until they arrive. My household duties will have to wait."

Caterina turns to her daughters.

"Bice, you and Ginevra go along and do what you can to oversee the servants in my absence. If I am needed into the night, Consolata will prepare a cot for me. She can bring the small one from the guest room."

"Wife," Piero adds, "I am returning to my studio immediately and will dispatch Matteo to both Father Giuseppe and Maestro Moyse right away. You girls come with me. The servants can wait. Go to your sister Marietta who is in the chapel and join her in prayer. Pray to Our Mother Mary to intercede. Perhaps God may hear her and give us some hope."

Before Piero leaves the room, he steps forward from the door where he has been standing and joins his wife by the bed. He reaches out his hand and gently covers Simonetta's right hand.

"My daughter, all in our family love you and will care for you as your own dear mother would. As I see you are in sore need of her consolation, I will send for her today so she can nurse you in your recovery. We all pray that your recovery will be speedy and go easily.

"I am your humble servant and will do all that is in my power to restore you to your former health and vivacity. Please accept my efforts as a token of my affection for you, my only son's beloved wife."

Caterina listens attentively to what Piero is half whispering to Simonetta. She has never heard his voice as tender, not even in the early days of their marriage when he made his clumsy attempts at expressing his love for her. A spark of jealousy flares in her as she thinks of how little affection Piero has given his own daughters. But Caterina

178

is a forgiving woman. One who loves Simonetta as if she were her own daughter even though she rarely shows her affection. The Vespucci are a strict and somber family.

A tear runs down Caterina's cheek. She does not understand whether it is for the tenderness she has witnessed in Piero or the feebleness that she has observed in Simonetta. Perhaps it is even for the remorse she feels that she has been a stranger to Piero's affections for all these years.

Piero places his hand over Simonetta's again.

"I leave you now to attend to the many letters I must write. But first, I will stop by the chapel to join my daughters in a prayer for your recovery."

After Piero has left the room followed by his two daughters, Consolata slowly releases Simonetta from her grasp. Simonetta, without saying a word, lies down and pulls the covers up over her head.

"Please be most attentive, Consolata. I will go and see to her breakfast and return as quickly as possible to sit with her while she eats and until the priest arrives."

"Yes, Madonna. I will not let her take one breathe without my notice. We are almost one these days. These last few nights, I have been sleeping on a pallet beside her bed. She has been more and more restless and is coughing without cease. I arise many times in the night to exchange the handkerchiefs she has used. They are covered in blood. I am so fearful of what is happening to her. The doctors' medicines have made no difference in these last days. I think she continues to grow worse."

Consolata buries her face in her hands.

"Do not despair, Consolata," Caterina takes a deep breath and continues. "Simonetta is still young and there are other doctors who perhaps know more than those who have already seen her. I will talk to Piero about calling Maestro Ficino. He is the most esteemed doctor in Florence and the father of Marsilio, her valued friend. I am sure he will be capable of finding a potion that will cure this cough she has developed.

"The blood she spits up must surely be from the irritation she has caused in her throat with all her coughing. I have seen this happen before. My own mother had a spell which lasted several months when she was unwell in a similar manner. She then recovered. We must not give up hope, my dear Consolata, but keep praying for her recovery."

As soon as Caterina closes the door behind her, Simonetta lowers the covers and turns to Consolata. Gasping for breath, she begins in a whisper, "Has there been any word from Giuliano today? I am puzzled he has not sent word round. He should have arrived two days ago and now another day has passed without any news. I am praying to Our Lady that he is safe. I am praying even harder that he has not forgotten me in his joy at returning."

"Oh, my lady, I am sure that he has not forgotten you. He loves you with all his heart. Has he not refused to marry? So many times that Lorenzo grows impatient with him. And he would not accept the Cardinalship, which meant eventually becoming Pope, because it would take him to Rome and away from you.

"Please do not distress yourself over the delay. I wager we will hear today. The courier has not yet arrived and when he does, I am convinced he will bring a letter from Giuliano with a very good reason for his delay in coming.

"Now rest, my sweet one. Today will prove to be a very trying day, what with the visits of Maestro Moyse and Father Giuseppe. And possibly even Giuliano. You will need your strength.

21

Less than an hour later when Piero arrives with Father Giuseppe, he finds the three women almost as he left them. The priest advances directly to the bed, but Piero stands just inside the door, as if his presence could jeopardize what is about to happen.

"Good day, Father Giuseppe." Caterina rises, puts down her needlework and comes forward to make a small bow and extend her hand.

"Signor Vespucci and I are extremely grateful you have come so soon. I am most concerned for the state of Simonetta's soul. Each night she has terrifying dreams in which she sees her most beloved Giuliano de' Medici threatened. Of course I cannot know the cause of these demonic dreams. I would venture that she fears something will happen to him or to il Magnifico while they are away in Pisa because of what she believes to be her own sins. I pray that by hearing her confession, you may cleanse her of these torments so she can find peace."

"My most honorable Madonna Vespucci, I will pray for God's help as I hear Simonetta's confession. I am sure He will grant us this benevolence I will pray that Simonetta is delivered from these demons which haunt her, and perhaps when she has found peace in her soul, her body will find its peace as well."

The priest continues. "With your leave, I will begin my ministrations now. Consolata may stay with me. I will come down to you when I have finished. Will I find you in your chapel?"

"Yes, of course, Father. Should you need me, Consolata can come for me."

As Caterina takes her leave, Father Giuseppe gently takes Simonetta's hand. He is a humble man as is the creed of his order, the Umiliata. When Simonetta opens her eyes to look at him, she smiles at seeing the same familiar face and slightly stooped shoulders that she has known since she first came to Florence. The sight of Father Giuseppe walking across the cobblestones of Ognissanti Piazza and down along the Arno has always been a reassurance to her that God's presence is still here on earth.

Then Simonetta closes her eyes for a moment and when she opens them again, she asks, "Is that you, Piero?"

"No, my child. I am Father Giuseppe. You know me well, and I, you. You have come to confession many times with me at Ognissanti. Today I have come to hear your confession and to give you my blessing and the blessing of Christ. Tell me your sins, my child, and I will offer them up to heaven for forgiveness."

"Please forgive me, Father Giuseppe. I thought for a moment you were my father-in-law. I am happy you have come, Father. I have much to confess and it weighs heavily on me. You have heard my confession many times before and my sins are always the same, but it will give me solace to confess them again."

Simonetta tries to pull herself up a bit in the bed. As she elevates her head slightly on the pillows, she begins slowly.

"My dear Father, again I confess my greatest sin. I have the sin of adultery in my heart. I love Giuliano de' Medici with all my heart. I love him as a real person, a real body, a real soul. That is my unforgivable transgression. To love one who is not my husband with my body and soul, and not just with my mind. I commit this sin over and over each day in my thoughts and in my imaginings. I commit it each night in my dreams. I am possessed, as if by the Devil. May God forgive me."

"Bless you, my child."

"I also have the sin of not obeying my husband as the Commandments require. I am not obedient to him because I do not respect the life that he lives. As the months pass, my devotion to him becomes less and less."

"Bless you, my child."

"I have the sin of envy in my heart. I have prayed to Our Lady that I may bear fruit, but I have never been with child. I envy those women who are fertile and who can give

God's gift of life to a child. I sometimes pretend my womb is full. That I carry Giuliano's child. I imagine his birth, the look of joy on his father's face, the bliss I will feel at holding him in my arms. And then I remember that I am not with child. It is then that I must also bear the sin of self loathing.

"Bless you, my child."

"I have the sin of lying to others about how ill I am. I am not honest about my despair or my fears. I do not want to distress those who care for me, so I hold all my anguish inside and tell many of those who love me that I am not afraid.

"Worst of all, Father, I do not trust God with all my heart. I am afraid He will let me die without seeing my beloved again. My desire for Giuliano is a sin against God and the Church. But my love for Giuliano is pure: it is love for the person he is and it is not a love forced by wealth, position, or convention. I know his love for me is the same.

"Bless you, my child."

"Father, I do not understand why a love so pure is not also a chaste love, blessed by Our Heavenly Father. My greatest fear is that He will not forgive me this transgression which has become the essence of my life. Can you promise me He will accept me into His presence should I die?"

Before Father Giuseppe can respond, Simonetta continues.

"I am so terribly afraid of dying, Father. I do not want God's Will to be done if Our Heavenly Father wants to take me from this world. Please, Father, tell me that God is a loving and forgiving God and that He will forgive me my waywardness. Assure me you will intercede for me and that God will receive me as his daughter."

"My child, I cannot ascertain what God will think or do. I can only intercede with Him on your behalf. I can only tell Him that your heart is free from hatred. That your love has been given freely. That you have sinned against the laws of God as they are written by men, but that you have not sinned against the laws of love. From my study of the past, I know that men have seen the laws of God differently in other times, in other places. Quite possibly, men will look at these present laws and understand God's nature differently in the future.

"But, my child, we must dwell in the present. I will pray for your soul. I will absolve you from your sins. I sentence you to say one hundred *Hail Marys* and admonish you to direct your mind, your eyes, and your body away from this love which is frowned upon by the Church.

"May God bless you, my child. As you have confessed your sins, may you find peace in your heart.

"And now, my dear, I must take my leave of you. May God be with you. May Christ be with you. May He cause His light to shine upon you and give you Peace. My Peace I leave with you.

"I will come again tomorrow after the morning mass to offer you the Holy Sacrament and to minister to you again, my most precious child of God. My dear Simonetta."

"Thank you, Father. I will try to find peace in your

words and in saying my *Hail Marys*. I will pray to Our Lady that I will soon be able to attend mass again at Ognissanti. Your visit has given me hope. I await your next visit with great anticipation. Please come whenever you can. Being in your presence gives me much comfort."

As the priest leaves the room, Simonetta turns her face from the door. Tears are running down her cheeks. Before she can wipe them away, she falls into another deep sleep.

22

The late afternoon sun comes in at a slant through the open windows. In winter, there is very little light at all, but toward the beginning of spring, the sun gives a soft warm light as it edges into the room and spills its gold onto the ceramic relief of Mary with the Christ Child which hangs over the cassone on the wall beside Simonetta's bed.

Consolata sits in one of the chairs she had brought up several days ago from the storehouse below so visitors might sit should they desire. Consi has never sat this way before, like a lady with her hands folded in her lap. Not even once throughout all the hours she has spent quietly watching over Simonetta in these last days. She, too, has her memories of Portovenere and Piombino. As she sits quietly in this room that seems unbearably empty when Simonetta is sleeping, these memories come back to her quite easily.

When she first came into the Cattaneo family household in Fezzano, she had been only four and so lonely for her own family that she passed her nights on her pallet beside Simonetta crying softly to herself, wishing she were again running the hills with her brothers. Night after night, she tried to understand why she, still almost a baby and the youngest girl in her family of struggling contadini, should be sent away from the only ones she had ever loved.

Her mother loved her. Of that she was sure.

Perhaps her mother had been wiser and more experienced than she had realized. Perhaps her parents had been right. Perhaps she had been happier and more cared for in the sprawling boisterous Cattaneo family than she would have been in her own family, doing without many necessities and then facing life as the deprived wife of another poor farmer.

These justifications she could fabricate for herself after all these years, but in those early years away from the love of all she had known as a very young child, she thought only of trying to hide her sadness, both from Simonetta and from herself.

Madonna Catocchia had been kind to her, spoiling her with little gifts and special treats to eat. She tried to feel as if this house at Fezzano, so strange to her at the time, were her home. Little by little, she had grown to love Simonetta as a sister. She had loved her soft voice, her quiet manner, her constant concern to include her "Consi" in everything she did. They had always played together as friends, even though Consolata knew her position was almost as lowly as a servant.

Later at Piombino, they were each other's best

friend. Two adolescents whispering and giggling together as if they were identical twins. Covertly spying on the servant boys. Making up their own criteria for judging each one. Trying out their skills at flirting whenever they thought they wouldn't be noticed. At Piombino, Consolata no longer cried at night, although she was much further from her family than ever. In fact by that time it had been so long since she had left her own family that she had begun to think of Simonetta as her only family,

She had been fortunate. When Simonetta was betrothed, Madonna Catocchia had decided the best place for Consolata was with Simonetta. Simonetta was Catocchia's youngest child, her baby, and she could not abide the thought that her child would not take with her some of the comfort and company from home. That the child of her heart might be lonely among strangers.

Now it is she, Consolata, not Catocchia, who is trying to keep Simonetta from being sad, who stays by her side to make her feel included in this life that has become less and less real for her each day.

While Consolata is still reminiscing, Simonetta begins coughing. This time the coughing is more desperate and frightfully forceful. Even though she does not seem to be awake, Simonetta leans up slightly and begins coughing into her hand. Consolata can see that there is blood again this time. She rises from her seat and goes to Simonetta with a linen towel. Gently she wipes the blood from her palm and places a clean handkerchief over it.

Simonetta does not open her eyes. She does not sit up any further. She gives several more violent coughs then falls back onto her pillows, appearing exhausted but still asleep. Consolata sits patiently beside her.

Simonetta is struggling to understand where she is.

As I look around me I realize I am walking through the San Lorenzo marketplace. It is hot and I am sweating. My clothes are drenched with perspiration, but I do not care.

In the distance, I can see Giuliano in the front of a cortege. The only thing I can think of is running to catch up with him. I am desperate to work my way through the crowd to his side. I struggle to get my breath. I feel as if I am climbing up a hill with the trees on every side lashing out at me, slowing my progress and burning my skin. I have to stop to catch my breath so often I think I must be running backward, for Giuliano is progressing further and further ahead of me.

Finally I realize I will never catch him. I stop to catch my breath once more, and it is then that I see what Giuliano is following. A bier. On the bier is the body of a young girl dressed all in white, with her gowns flowing down over the sides and floating slightly with the breeze.

I try to approach the bier, rising above the crowds, hearing their dirge. As I hover over the crowd, I can see quite clearly. The cortege has stopped and Giuliano is prostrate, kneeling just behind the carriage. His grief has turned his face into that of an old man, though his body is still young.

Resolutely I move my eyes to the figure on the bier. I am preternaturally calm. I have separated myself from any fear or grief as I look into the uncovered face of the corpse on the bier. The face is that of a beautiful young girl, an exquisite face even in death.

I am looking into my own face.

I do not understand why I am in the market place before the Church of San Lorenzo, looking at my own body on a bier, seeing my own face. I begin to hear a rapping sound.

Consolata arises and goes to the door. Biattina stands there with a letter in her hand.

"Senor Vespucci asked me to bring this letter to you. It is for Madonna Simonetta. He said she will be so happy to receive it. You can see the seal is broken. He said to tell Madonna that it was broken by accident when the courier was handing it to Giorgio. He sends his apologies."

As she hands the letter to Consolata, Biattina has a knowing look on her face. She and Consolata both know that this was not the first time a letter had "accidentally" been opened before it was placed in Simonetta's hands.

Simonetta pulls herself quickly from her dream. She has heard what Biattina said, but this time she does not care if Piero has opened her mail. All she wants is to know what has happened to Giuliano. When she will see him. If only he would come today.

Consolata brings the letter directly to the bedside.

"Would you like me to help you sit up in bed, my lady."

"No, Consi, thank you. I have been waiting for so long, I cannot wait another second. I will just lie here. The light is strong enough. Stay here beside me as I read."

23

My most treasured and beloved Simonetta,

How it brings tears to my eyes to think that I was not able to come to you directly upon arriving in Florence. As you may have calculated, we returned very late and extremely spent last night, the 24th. My mother was awaiting our arrival with disturbing news.

There has been an outbreak of an influenza which some call the Plague in the hills above Florence and it has infected several of the servants at the villas Cafaggiolo and Trebbio. Luckily, Careggi has been spared. My mother is hoping that the outbreak can be contained, but she feels that she must send me directly with a party of servants, her instructions and supplies for the sick. She believes that the use of certain herbs as a cleansing medium will keep the contagion from spreading. Her healing powers and knowledge are most respected among the peasants, so she has been able to do much in the past to help in such an event. Since she is suffering terribly from her arthritis in this moment, I cannot refuse to head this mission of mercy for her.

One of our doctors will accompany me. We will leave later this morning after the servants have finished loading the supplies and we will return tomorrow evening. The trip will be arduous as I will be pushing both men and horses to travel from villa to villa as quickly as possible so as not to delay my return to Florence on the 26th and to you on the 27th. Even though I will be overly occupied every minute, it will seem years.

I have a great surprise for you! I have brought back with me a good supply of Vermentino, your favorite white wine from Portovenere. Now, our little jewel of a wine cellar at Careggi will be well stocked with this treasure. A secret we will not share with many, I hope. When I wrote your mother to ask if she would like to send something back to you, right away she sent her man to Pisa with several barrels from your brother's vineyards.

How delightful it will be to drink this wine with you after it has settled in the cave for a few weeks. Early summer will be the perfect time for its tartness, chilled to a temperature of frost.

Where shall we drink it? There at the table in the grotto among the beautiful mosaics? Or perhaps on the loggia, overlooking the valley, talking of our past times together there? Maybe we should run away to our secret glen where we have often spread out our woolen capes, lying on them trying to imitate the reclining position the Caesars perfected. And laughing the whole time. The reveries I have of our last encounter there will last me for my lifetime. But, of course, I am holding my breath in anticipation of replacing those memories with some which are more recent and, dare I dream the impossible, more ardent.

In only a few more hours, I will hold you in my arms again. I will kiss your mouth so roundly you will need to sit down to recover from the force of it. I will kiss your cheeks, your neck, your wrists, your ankles, the backs of your knees, all of you until you beg to be set free for fear you will never again catch your breath.

The days have been long without you. But there are only two short days until we will be together again. I will not wait to send word; I will simply appear in the early hours of the morning on the 27th and serenade you from beneath your window. The first song you will hear after the song of the lark will be my song of joy at being so near you.

Please forgive me that this letter is short and comes after you were expecting me in person. I have tried to send it as quickly as possible after I realized I would not be able to come today.

I remain your servant, smitten with love for you and impatient to be in your arms again.

May the Almighty keep you in health,
Your Giuli
From Via Largo
25 April 1476

24

No ! No ! No!

I hear myself scream as I stand upright in the pew.

"Stop! This madness must stop!"

I can not believe the horror before my eyes. Knives are flashing to the right and left of the main altar. Everything is in chaos. The crowds near the altar begin screaming and fighting to get to the side doors. The Cathedral is full of Easter Sunday worshipers, but for most there is no way to know what is happening. People are frantic in their attempts to understand. They are panicked and determined to escape whatever disaster is occurring.

Bernardo Bandini brings down his knife with great force, crying, "Here, Traitor!"

"Help him! Help him! Someone please help Giuliano!" I hear myself screaming.

I see Giuliano stagger backwards as Francesco de' Pazzi raises his knife with such a furor that I myself draw back. Over and over he raises his knife, each time striking closer and closer to the floor.

On the other side of the altar, two priests are heading toward Lorenzo. One grabs him by the shoulders and raises his arm over him. It takes me a few seconds to realize that the priest, too, has a dagger and that he is poised to deliver a blow to Lorenzo. Lorenzo is struck and stumbles back, covering his neck with his cloak.

I shriek. I can no longer find any words. I can no longer call for help. I can only try to make my scream heard over the din in the cathedral. Over the scene from hell I am witnessing.

Michelino's fresco depicting Dante's Inferno *flashes through my mind. On all sides of me devils with their raised swords pursue the wicked into the abode of the damned. Except that Lorenzo and Giuliano are not the wicked. I cannot make sense of this scene before me, my inferno.*

Lorenzo beats back his attackers as his friends close in around him to guide him across the altar to the doors of the New Sacristy. I see his friend Nori following him, trying to stave off Bandini who is in pursuit of Lorenzo. I gasp as I see Bandini run his sword through Nori's stomach. Nori crumples onto the marble tiles. The delay from this attack is enough to allow Lorenzo to reach the safety of the Sacristy. Poliziano quickly closes and bolts the doors behind them.

I cannot see Giuliano. I am unable to move. Even though almost everyone else in the cathedral has fled, I remain. I am the sole figure still standing in the pews. A few shadowy figures with knives are creeping up the side aisles toward the altar.

Suddenly Francesco de' Pazzi leaves the spot where he has been standing over Giuliano, moving as if he is exhausted from the tremendous effort he has made. He has stabbed Giuliano over and over, like a madman attacking his foe without reason.

As Francesco starts for the door of the Sacristy, I can suddenly see the north side of the apse clearly. In the space which Francesco has deserted, I see the body of my beloved Giuliano lying on the marble, covered with blood and not moving. Through the dome window, the light emanating from Donatello's Coronation of the Virgin *shines directly down on Giuliano's body, the white of Mary's skirt illuminating his face, the red of Christ's robe brightening the blood on Giuliano's chest.*

I fall to my knees and I pray to God as I have never prayed before.

"Heavenly Father, please help me. Hear my confession. Hear my promise to you.

"Father, I know my greatest sin is not the one the Church has seen and overlooked. It is not the one all of Florence has applauded. It is not my betrayal of my husband, Marco. No, none of these. My real sin is that I have loved Giuliano de' Medici. Not in the Platonic sense of perfect love, the love of beauty, the love of God, but in the real sense. I have loved him as a real person, a real body, a real soul. I have loved him more than You, Heavenly Father. I now know that is my unforgivable transgression. That is my greatest sin.

"Dearest Heavenly Father, I promise that if you will save Giuliano, I will give my own life in return. I will find a way to stop loving him, for not loving him is to me the same as not living. Please, Heavenly Father, hear my plea. Amen."

25

Panicked by the gruesome scene she has just witnessed and terrified that her prayer will not be enough to save Giuliano, Simonetta begins coughing. She cannot stop the violent spasms, the gasping for breath, the blood she sees on the linen kerchief Consolata has given her.

Consolata rises quickly, takes up the expectorant from the table and goes to the bedside.

"Here, my lady, take a spoonful of this horrible tasting concoction. It will ease the coughing."

Simonetta is very weak, but raises her head just enough to allow Consolata to pour a little syrup in her mouth. As the coughing eases, she takes a deep breath and tries to sleep again. The fear she felt during the nightmare of Giuliano's assassination has not left her. She cannot dispel the picture of him lying on the marble floor of the cathedral, his tunic bloodied with so many wounds she cannot count them all. Refuses to count them.

As she settles into a more comfortable position, she

is aware that her shift is wet and cold. She huddles under the pile of coverlets that surrounds her. After her body warms again, she falls into a fitful sleep.

I can feel the sun on my face, but there are tears on my cheeks. As I am walking down Borgo San Lorenzo, I see throngs along the road, among them many people I know. There is Jacopo, the jeweler at the Mercato San Lorenzo. And there is the leatherworker, Dominico, from Santa Croce, who makes our books. Our courier. They are all standing along the road, each with his head bowed, his eyes lowered, a look of anguish on his face.

Ahead of me are the members of the Medici family following a carriage. Directly behind the carriage is Lucrezia with her arm in Lorenzo's. Following behind them are Lorenzo's brothers and sisters. Then Clarice and her children. But where is Giuliano? I dare not let my eyes wander from the family to search for him. I do not want to know what I might discover.

Forcing myself to be courageous, I raise my eyes to look at the burden the carriage is carrying. At first I cannot see what is atop the gilded carriage because of the heavy dust. Then at last I see what is there. It is a bier. The body on it is covered by a veil of black silk with gold edging which falls over the top of the carriage. A gold embroidered Medici family Coat of Arms is centered on the body.

I am confused by what I am seeing. But as I continue to stare at the carriage, I see at last that the body on the bier is my Giuli. I stumble forward, not daring to raise my head. If Giuli is dead, my life, too, is ended. I am numb. I cannot move or think.

But I do move. I arouse myself from my deep sleep and this dire dream. I have heard a noise in the courtyard outside. Is it

200

possible that Giuli has come in the dead of night to search me out?

Slowly I pull back the covers and slip from the bed, being careful not to disturb Consi who is sleeping beside me on the trundle bed. I tiptoe to the window and there in the moonlight that floods the courtyard I can make out a figure, one I know very well. I cannot believe what I am seeing. Giuliano. My Giuli. He must see my figure in the window, for he waves and then jumps down from his horse and waves again.

Not since my first encounter with Giuliano at Via Largo have I felt such eagerness. I wave from the window, then step down, go to the cassone and take out my woolen cape. I put on the slippers that are on the step beside my bed. Impetuous as I am, I am not so impetuous as to go unprotected out into the damp and chilly night air. Not even for Giuliano, I tell myself, although these few seconds it takes to arm myself feel like a full day of hours and minutes.

I am shaking. I am weak, but the joy I feel makes my heart beat faster. My whole body is responding to the call to go to Giuliano.

I am cautious opening the door so as not to wake Consolata after all. I close it behind me, careful not to let the latch click even though my impatience makes me want to fling the door wide and leave it unclosed while I run down the steps.

He has come at last. He has come even though he is not expected until morning. He has come to give me the strength I have been lacking since his departure. I cannot wait to be held in his arms again. To feel his warmth, to smell his scent.

As I hurry down the stairs, the light of the moon through the window is scattered along the tiles leading to the entrance door.

It is almost as if Giuliano himself were emanating light.

As I open the great door, the light becomes brighter. It shines directly on Giuliano as he waits for me. How many weeks I have been longing for this moment! I almost stumble in my rush to run to him as he comes toward me with his arms outstretched.

The moon shines all around us. Even the cobblestones glitter with its radiance. Giuliano folds me in his arms, then covers my face with eager kisses. Softening his lips on mine, he lets them communicate all the love he is feeling.

Without a word, Giuliano takes me up in his arms and sets me on the back of his horse, swinging himself up in front of me with one swift movement. Although I am shaking, whether from the cold or from weakness, I simply let myself melt into his back as I ease my arms around him, already seeing all those beautiful moments we have spent together spread out before me like the most voluptuous banquet table.

As if knowing what is to happen, the horse turns around and heads out the gates of the courtyard down Via del Porcellana toward Santa Maria Novella. Past the square and the church, through the Porto a Faenza and up the road toward Careggi.

The further we ride, the more I feel at peace. The heaviness of my body disappears. The coughing stops. I no longer sense my weakness or even the cold. In fact, I feel as though I am leaving my earthly body behind and assuming a heavenly one. As we ride, the road before us is luminescent.

Soon I see Careggi in the distance. My soul's home. I imagine walking through the gardens embraced by the moonlight, Giuliano's arm about my waist. Just the two of us together until the dawn breaks over the valley and brings the entire world to life.

A corridor of light covers the cypress trees lining both sides of the road. It guides us and intensifies as we draw closer to the villa. Here we have first known each other. Here we have spent our happiest moments. Here I have felt only contentment and peace.

As we enter the gates, the brightness becomes almost unbearable. It illuminates everything around us. As its radiance envelops me too, I know I am where I should be. My whole being is one with Giuliano. My whole being is one with God. My whole being is Love.

From *The Book of the Dead 1475 - 1487*
26 Aprile 1476. E morta La Simonetta.

Part V

27 April 1476

To our most venerated Magnifico,

     The beautiful soul of Simonetta has been given up to Paradise, which you have no doubt already heard. One can say that Death has triumphed a second time for, in truth, if you could have seen her after her death, she would not have seemed to you any less beautiful or less charming than during her lifetime.
     Requiescat in Pace!

Your most humble servant,
Sforza Bettini
27 April 1476

26

Giuliano de' Medici awakes with a start to the sound of pounding horse's hooves on the road leading up to the entrance gate to Careggi. The sun is barely peaking through the shutters, but it is bright enough for him to know dawn has already come.

Quickly Giuliano throws on his boots and runs down the stairs to the courtyard to greet Poliziano. By the sound of the hooves he is certain who is coming at such a breakneck speed. He thinks immediately the news must be about his mother who is rarely in good health these days and whose frequent journeys around the countryside have made her vulnerable to any pestilence that might be spreading in the villages beyond Florence.

Poliziano rides directly into the courtyard, ducking his head at the doors which have already been opened by the gatekeeper. He pulls the horse upright just beside the well, both horse and rider panting loudly, and swings down without so much as a raise of his hand.

Giuliano knows Angelo's haste must be for good reason. When Angelo stands before him, he knows the news must be wretched. Angelo bends his head slightly to catch his breath, then firmly grasps both Giuliano's shoulders with his gloved hands. He says solemnly, "The news I bring you is the worst that you could ever imagine. Please, my friend, trust in God that it is his will. Otherwise, neither of us will be able to survive."

Without hesitating, Poliziano continues. "La Bella has gone to her Heavenly home. She left us during the night. Consolata heard Simonetta calling your name, over and over as if she were riding off with you on your great white stallion as she often dreamt of doing so. When Consolata rose to check on her, she found her body so calm she thought Simonetta was having the most tranquil sleep, the kind she used to have when she was a little girl at Portovenere. Her beatific smile exuded peace and love. Only when Consolata bent over her more closely to hear her breathing did she realize Simonetta was not asleep, but had stopped all earthly breathe.

"My dear friend, I am destroyed that I must bring you this news. I am overcome with grief at the loss of this beauteous spirit who is my muse and my only touch with love. I am besotted with grief."

Poliziano falls to his knees on the rough pebbles of the courtyard, covers his face with his hands, and begins to sob uncontrollably.

Giuliano does not go to him. He remains on the

212

bench where he has stumbled when he first heard the words, *La Bella.*

He did not need to hear more. He was struck down. He did not even cry out, or sink to his knees, or begin to sob. He stared straight at the well, never blinking until Angelo had finished speaking and had dropped to his knees.

As if on command, Giuliano rises, takes the reigns of Poliziano's horse, throws himself up on it and gives its sides a kick. The horse is quick to respond as if he knows that this will be his most important ride. He does not even look back at his master. He knows the new rider well enough to know he must obey him.

Giuliano rides like a madman through the gates, down the entrance drive and out onto the road that leads to Florence. The sun is now fully up over the hills to the East. The road is filled with farmers taking their produce to market. With artisans taking their goods to the city. Giuliano sees none of this. He rides past all at a gallop, never slowing, barely missing carts and women walking on the road, gaining speed with every stride of the horse. Not even in a joust has he ridden so fiercely and so well.

As he rides through Porto a Faenza, Giuliano senses a pall over the city. Everyone he passes bows as if a king is passing on the day of his greatest defeat. But his expression does not change. He rides straight down the Via Faenza to San Lorenzo, his parish church. The crowds which are already gathered around the church make way for him as he passes and turns down the road that leads directly to the Borgo Ognissanti. The little children along the way get down on their knees and bow their heads. There is not a sound as Giuliano passes, but behind him, echoes of grief.

Giuliano rides directly into the courtyard of the Vespucci house on Ognissanti. He stops his horse abruptly, looks up at Simonetta's window and wails. So loud and so mournful is the sound that all along the road shutters are thrown open and women appear in the windows, bearing first a look of curiosity and then a reflection of Giuliano's grief.

Giuliano does not get down from his horse. He sits in the middle of the courtyard with his head bowed, moaning with a sound so doleful that those who hear it will remember it for the rest of their lives.

Within a few minutes, Piero appears in the doorway, holding in his hand the crucifix he has been using for his supplications. It is clear that he does not know what to do when he sees Giuliano, although he lowers his head and moves toward him. Still Giuliano does not move, does not say a word.

"Your most Honorable Grace, I offer you my most genuine condolences and those of my family. We are all devastated by the loss of the fairest lady to have walked this earth. We have done nothing but cry out in agony since Consolata first brought us the news this morning. Please accept our most sincere sympathies and know that we did everything possible to save her. No one realized that she was so near death, not even the doctors who attended her. There

214

is nothing more I knew to do. Her mother did not realize she should come right away and other doctors here did not want to interfere with Lorenzo's doctor. We were beside ourselves in knowing how to care for her…"

Giuliano raises his right hand slowly in a gesture that causes Piero to stop his rambling. He sits perfectly still in the same position as when he arrived. Finally he raises his eyes and looks down to meet those of Piero.

"May I see her?" he asks.

"Oh, Your Grace. Would that you could. She is being prepared for her funeral which is arranged for later this morning. You will have the place of honor in the cortege, directly behind the bier. The way is short from here to the Church. There will be little room along the streets for all of the people that have gathered."

Giuliano hesitates some time before responding to Piero. He is trying to emerge from the depths of his grief and focus on his duty.

"Signor Vespucci, I respectfully request that the cortege pass first by our family church of San Lorenzo. So many people are waiting there to pay their respects that the streets around it are already crowded with the mourning. If the cortege passes by them, the whole city will know that Lorenzo is here in spirit. He will surely feel honored and pleased that you have given him a part in the burial."

"I will arrange it, your honor. How weighty my burden as her protector has been. I have administered to her needs as I would have to those of my own children.

Have cared for her tribulations on this earth. I do not wish to relinquish my post, but I am content she will soon pass into the hands of her Heavenly Father where she will be at peace. Please come with me, Signore."

Giuliano dismounts. Without a word, he follows Piero into the house to await the moment when he can finally see his love. He sits in Piero's study watching a mourning dove fly back and forth from a myrtle tree to a nest on the ledge of Simonetta's window. He is bringing food to his mate. Giuliano can hear the chirping of the chicks through the open window.

Each sound brings new grief to him and he can not stop the loud sobs which escape through his hands which he has placed over his face. He thinks of the dreams he has had for the future; playing with his own children at Careggi, delighting in them as Lorenzo does in his. Little games of Hide and Seek or Blind Man's Bluff. His beautiful Simonetta dancing among them, laughing and calling out, her skirts billowing around her, her glorious eyes covered with his silk handkerchief.

A loud clang startles Giuliano out of his reverie. The priests have entered the courtyard, the bells have begun to peal, the family is gathering in the passageway. Giuliano feels removed from everything around him. It is as if he were not there in body, but watching everything from some distant place. From his position at Piero's window, he can not see everything that is going on, but somehow he knows exactly how each little sound translates into some action.

He remembers the day his father was buried. How each part of that day seemed surreal. And yet on that day, he had had a part to play and he had played it well.

Today he is no longer an actor strutting about, doing his duty. Today he is totally human. He is totally defeated. He is without reason to go on living. All he has lived for, all he has dreamt of, all he loves has been taken from him. The most beautiful, graceful spirit that God has ever made is upstairs in this house, lying on a bed he has never known, all breath gone out of her body.

Piero enters the study with a close friend of the Medici, Nicolo Martelli, whose head is bowed.

"You may go up to see her now," Nicolo says quietly.

Giuliano does not even look up at him. He mutters into his hands, "I am the most unhappy of men. I no longer am in possession of my wits, nor of my life. I live because God wills me to live, not because I will it. I cannot bear to see her lying on a bed as if she were still alive and she is not. Better that I see her borne out into the courtyard where there will be many to help me sustain the knowledge that she no longer lives. I am destroyed. My life no longer has meaning. I will need to garner whatever life is left to me from others, from my brother, my mother, my friends. The Giuliano de' Medici the world knew is no longer."

As the two men leave the room, closing the door behind them, Giuliano has already retreated into his grief. He sits unmoving for almost an hour before Piero enters again, a large bundle wrapped in black velvet held out on both arms. Giuliano lifts his head to regard Piero, his eyes glazed over and his face ashen.

"I have had Consolata prepare for you some of Simonetta's belongings. Here you will find the dress she wore for your joust, the banner Lorenzo had made for you, a small portrait of her I commissioned Leonardo da Vinci to make for me, and the two brooches you gave her which she wore almost always. I will have these things sent round to Via Largo. They will be waiting for you there."

Piero continues in a quiet voice. "Your Grace, Consolata assures me that with her last breath, Simonetta called to you as if she were riding behind you on her way to Careggi, smiling as she always did when she was most happy."

Giuliano nods and returns to his grief. He does not raise his head again even as he follows Piero and his family out to the courtyard where Simonetta's bier has already been lifted onto the shoulders of the other men of the Vespucci family.

From the house for the entire length of the cortege, the casket is carried open so that all who gathered to see her were moved to copious tears. Of all of these, some had nothing to say and others had a compassion born of admiration that she, in death, had a beauty more superlative than in life, which beauty seemed unsurpassable. In those who had not known her there is born a dolor and a remorse not to have known one so beautiful who was open to all and therefore they are in perpetual sadness. Truly in her is verified that which our Petrarch has said: "Death appears beautiful on her beautiful face."

From *Commento* by Lorenzo de' Medici

27

Simonetta is dressed in a white voile morning shift covered by a white silk cloak so ethereal it spills over the sides of the bier and floats gently with each movement of the bearers. Ignoring all custom, her face has been left unveiled. She has never looked more beautiful.

As the cortege leaves the courtyard, those who have been standing around in silence trying to control their own grief fall in behind Giuliano who is unaware of where he is or who else is present.

The priests, for there were three of them, walk in front of the bier. The elders of the Vespucci family, Piero, Giorgio Antonio, Guido Antonio and Stagio, take their place behind Giuliano. Following them are the rest of the immediate family, the last of whom is Marco, giving deference to others on this occasion of Simonetta's death as he did during her life. Poliziano has the first place of honor after the family, followed by other members of the Accademia including Sandro Botticelli, Marsilio Ficino and Leonardo da Vinci. The list of Florentine notables is impossibly long.

Waiting in the Church of Ognissanti are even more illustrious members of society. Lucrezia de' Medici has come as a close friend as well as a representative of Lorenzo and the Medici family. Lorenzo's wife Clarice Orsini is also there. And the Tornabuoni family. Even Jacobo the elder of the Pazzi family waits in his pew, prepared to rise as the procession enters.

Giuliano's eyes are never lifted from the ground. His shoulders bear the grief of a thousand men. He has begun the interminable journey he had hoped never to make, the one from the world of the living to the world of the damned.

Control this intense furor which moves you,
your complaints will not trouble in the heaven,
she who has made your love divine.
She for whom you cry is not dead however.
She is alive, free of earthly bonds.
Reflect and know that she awaits you.

Bernardo Pulci

Sonnet I

Oh, shining star who by your radiance
Steals from your neighboring stars their light,
Why is your brilliance so much greater than ever?
Why do you wish to compete with Phoebus now?

Perhaps your beautiful eyes, taken from us
by cruel Death, who does presume too much,
are in you so welcoming: that adorned with their deity,
you may ask of Phoebus his beautiful chariot.

O this or newborn star that you are
Whose newfound splendor adorns the heavens,
grant, oh goddess, these our prayers:
Send us enough of your splendor
That our eyes, which for eternity would have wept fervently,
Without another tear will show you our happiness.

From *Il commento dei miei sonetti* by Lorenzo de' Medici

Epilogue

Madonna of the Pomegranate
Sandro Botticelli
(circa 1487)
tempera on panel
Collection of the Uffizi Museum
Florence

Simonetta Cattaneo -1453-1476

One of the most striking aspects about Simonetta Vespucci's story is, as mentioned in the Preface, there remain no first person documents from her. Although she was well educated, knew Latin and Greek, and participated in the gatherings of the most talented and scholarly men and women of Italian Renaissance, there are no letters written by or to her, no poems or translations done by her, nor any evidence that she wrote journals. Nor is there even one reference to any. However she is discussed in many of the documents of the period, especially those of members of the Accademia. Contemporary historians wrote most profusely about her especially during the epoch of Giuliano's tournament. For decades after her death, many of the most venerated scholars and poets of the time including Lorenzo de' Medici wrote sonnets, other poems, and made tributes to her in their journals and histories.

In addition to these writings, numerous paintings, sketches and banners with Simonetta's image were produced during her lifetime, and after her death artists still used her portrait in their paintings. Botticelli repeatedly used her face to depict that of the Madonna. He later said it was she whom he painted the rest of his life.

Presently, there is much controversy as to the accuracy of Simonetta's portrayal in the paintings of Botticelli and in those of other artists such as Piero di Cosimo whose well-known painting of her was done in

229

1480. Botticelli, in particular, increasingly seemed to have idealized her beauty as can be seen by comparing his sketch done shortly before her death with some of the later paintings, such as *The Birth of Venus* and *The Madonna of the Pomegranate*. Art critiques today hold the prevailing opinion that the longer the intervening years from the death of Simonetta in 1476 to the date of the painting, the more idealized her beauty becomes.

Woodcuts above and at right are from
La Giostra di Giuliano de Medici...
Written by Angelo Poliziano
(circa 1495–1500)
printed book with woodcut illustrations
Collection of Metropolitan Museum of Art
New York

LAGIOSTRA DI GIVLIANO DE MEDICI.

Giuliano de' Medici- 1453-1478

Exactly two years after the death of Simonetta, Giuliano de' Medici was assassinated in the Cathedral of Maria del Fiore, Il Duomo, at Florence, Italy on April 26, 1478, in what was to be called the Pazzi Conspiracy. He was stabbed 17 times according to most witnesses. The assailants were his so-called friends, Bernardo Bandini Baroncelli and Francesco de' Pazzi, who had gone to the Medici palace on Via Largo to escort him to the church that Easter morning after he had decided to stay at home and rest a wounded leg. They had joked with him in the street and jostled him to be sure he was not armed or protected by a shirt of chain mail under his clothing.

Four days later, Giuliano was interred in the family church of San Lorenzo. He had been a seasoned diplomat and had supported Lorenzo in his administration of the Republic. He was called "The Prince of Youth" during his lifetime and was admired and loved by most of Florence. He was widely mourned because of his many virtues and his lively and amicable spirit.

Giuliano de' Medici never married. He had refused to do so during the life of Simonetta, finding excuses not to finalize even the most advantageous marriage arrangement. He had also refused to take the Vatican position Lorenzo had arranged for him, that of Cardinal, which would have led to his being Pope.

A few days after Giuliano's death, Lucrezia de' Medici, his mother, found out that he had recently fathered an illegitimate child who had been born only a few months earlier. That child, Giulio de' Medici, named after his father, was taken into the Medici home and raised by Lorenzo along side his own children. Giuliano de' Medici's son subsequently became Pope Clement VII.

After the death of Giuliano, Poliziano never finished his verses on the tournament of Giuliano. However, he wrote many times about his best friend. In one passage he describes Giuliano's character and his own grief, giving

Giuliano the attributes of kindness, strength and virtue. He reflected that Giuliano's qualities had made him loved by all the people during his lifetime and mourned greatly after his death.

The notation "For the details of Giuliano's death..." was found in one of Lorenzo de' Medici's notebooks along with five pages left blank to be filled with his impressions. However, Lorenzo never returned to his journals to write of his brother's death.

Giuliano de' Medici
with Mourning Dove
Sandro Botticelli
1446–1510
tempera on panel
Collection of
National Gallery
of Art
Washington, D.C.

Bust of Lorenzo de' Medici
Andrea del Verrocchio
1478/1521
painted terracotta
Collection of National Gallery of Art
Washington, D.C.

Lorenzo de' Medici-1449-1492

Lorenzo de' Medici survived the assassination plot that took the life of his brother, Giuliano, on April 26, 1478. The Pazzi Conspiracy had failed to kill both brothers, which was its aim. All surviving members of the conspiracy as well as their families were jailed or banished from the city. No Florentine was allowed to marry into those families in exile. The major conspirators, including Archbishop Salviati, were killed, most by public hanging, many hanged naked from the Palazzo della Signoria. Lorenzo asked Botticelli to record this gruesome scene in a sketch which still exists. Other members of the conspiracy were tortured or mutilated by the Council of Eight or by the citizens loyal to Lorenzo, their bodies chopped to pieces or eaten by the dogs. All were refused burial.

Lorenzo maintained his control of the Republic. More in control than ever, he was more popular and had greater loyalty among its citizens. Although Lorenzo suffered from gout, as did his father, he continued his intellectual activities with the Accademia, wrote a detailed daily journal, paid great attention to the education of his children as well as to those whom he had adopted as his own. Those children included Michelangelo Buonarroti, the artist, and Giulio, the illegitimate son of his brother Giuliano.

Lorenzo supported the arts in an extravagant manner throughout his life. He financed the universities in the Republic and maintained peace and prosperity through his extraordinary diplomatic skills. Until her death in 1482, Lorenzo's mother, Lucrezia Tornabuoni de' Medici, aided Lorenzo in all phases of his life, including his intellectual and artistic pursuits and his political maneuvering.

Like his father and grandfather before him, Lorenzo spent more and more time at Careggi as he grew older. He died peacefully at the age of 43, April 8, 1492, in his own bedroom in Careggi. Several accounts say Savonarola administered the last rites, but that report is disputed today. It is known that he was surrounded by his lifelong friends and his family.

After one day of lying in state at the monastery of San Marco, Lorenzo was buried on April 10 at the church of San Lorenzo in the Medici Chapel alongside his brother, Giuliano. During the almost 23 years that Lorenzo il Magnifico was at its head, Florence flourished as the artistic, cultural, and literary center of Europe. Never, before or since, has a city seen such a combination of these attributes with such a high degree of excellence.

The Triumph of Fame
Birthplate of Lorenzo de' Medici
(reverse) Coat of Arms and other symbols
of the Medici and Tornabuoni Families
Giovanni di ser Giovanni Guidi
(circa 1449)
tempera, silver, and gold on wood
Collection of Metropolitan Gallery of Art
New York

Lucrezia Tornabuoni
Domenico Ghirlandaio
(circa 1475)
tempera and oil on panel
Collection of National Gallery of Art
Washington, D.C.

Lucrezia Tornabuoni de' Medici- 1425-1482

Lucrezia Tornibouni de' Medici was the multi-faceted and talented wife of Piero de' Medici and mother of Lorenzo il Magnifico. She was also one of the leading examples of the phenomena arising in the Renaissance called "The Other Voice," women who contributed significantly to dispelling the long held ideas that women were an inferior race and driven by their sexual urges. Lucrezia embraced the Platonic belief that men and women are equal in intellect and virtue. (Bless his heart and hers.)

In addition to running the many estates of the Medici and tending to the hundreds of family and servants, she was the de facto head of the Florentine government while her husband was ill and, later, when her son was away or otherwise occupied. She was a member of the Neo-Platonist Accademia. She translated from Greek and Latin, and she published several books of poetry as well as one for women on the running of the household. Her books and laudi, or religious poems, are still being translated, read and studied today. In her poetry, which was primarily religious in nature, she wrote poignantly about the history of sexual and societal abuse of women, especially in the Old Testament.

Until she died at the age of 57 in 1482, she continued to influence all phases of the Medici family life and to have an indisputable power in Florence, both on her own and through Lorenzo.

Sandro Botticelli - 1445-1510

Alessandro Filipepi, known as Sandro Botticelli, was born to Mariano di Vanni d'Amedeo Filipepi, a tanner, in 1445. The family lived in the Ognissanti quarter where their house abutted those of the Vespucci.

Sandro gained fame, first as a goldsmith, then later as one of the most innovative and sensitive painters the world has ever known. Hundreds of books have been written about his talent, his technique, and his extraordinary ability to capture the soul as well as the physical appearance of a person in his paintings. He was an intimate of the members of the Accademia.

We can infer that Botticelli knew Simonetta through the Accademia and as a familiar of the Vespucci family. Today, two paintings in particular link Botticelli to Simonetta, *The Birth of Venus* and *The Primavera*. Other of his paintings are known to be of Simonetta, among them several of Simonetta portrayed as the Madonna and some with Giuliano in scenes based on mythology.

Following his death, Botticelli was granted his request to be buried in the Vespucci chapel at Simonetta's feet. When the church of Ognissanti was reconstructed in the 17th century, the Vespucci chapel was moved and the tomb of Simonetta disappeared. Today, Botticelli's marble tombstone holds a prominent place centered on the floor of the new Vespucci chapel. There is no evidence anywhere of the tomb of Simonetta.

The Adoration of the Magi
Sandro Botticelli
(circa 1475–1476)
tempera on panel
Collection of the
Uffizi Museum
Florence

(Detail) Boticelli's Self
Portrait

Angelo Poliziano - 1454-1494

Angelo Poliziano, also called Angelo Ambrogini, was born in 1454, only one year after Simonetta, Giuliano, and Marco. He died two years after Lorenzo. Poliziano was one of the foremost scholars of the Renaissance. He translated the *Iliad* from Latin and various other significant literary works from Greek. His best known achievement

Medallion of Poliziano
Metropolitan Museum of Art
New York

is *Stanzas Begun on the Tournament of the Magnificent Giuliano de' Medici*, a poetic work in terza rima praising Giuliano and Simonetta in a mythological presentation. He completed Book I, but abandoned Book II after Giuliano's death.

Angelo was a constant companion of Giuliano as well as a tutor to him. He was in frequent correspondence with Lorenzo and Lucrezia de' Medici, helping them edit their works and assisting in the education of the household. He remained an intimate in the Medici household until after Giuliano's assassination. Later, a quarrel with Lorenzo's wife, Clarice, caused him to flee to Mantua. After several years, he returned to be the chair of Latin and Greek at the University of Florence, but never again lived in the Medici household.

Piero Vespucci- 1432-1485

Piero Vespucci was born into a prominent Florentine family esteemed for their contributions to Florentine society. Simone, Piero's grandfather, established Santa Maria dell'Umiltà hospital for the indigent sick. Piero's brother, Anastasio, the father of the navigator Amerigo Vespucci, built the Vespucci chapel in the Ognissanti church. He also commissioned Ghirlandaio and Botticelli to execute the two exquisite frescoes there, *Saint Jerome* and *Saint Augustine*. Another brother, Guido Antonio was judge emeritus and director of the school of letters at the University of Pisa. Lorenzo appointed him to several ambassadorships. The third brother was Giorgio Antonio. He was Canon of the city church, translating many Greek and Latin documents.

Piero, son of Giuliano di Piero, married Caterina Benci and had three daughters and one son. In his early years, he proved himself to be a good financier, sea captain, and importer. Later he was sent by Piero de' Medici as ambassador to various other kingdoms, including Piombino. There at the height of his influence, he arranged for the marriage of his son, Marco, to Simonetta Cattaneo in 1469. In 1470, he was sent by Lorenzo as ambassador to the court of Alfonso of Aragon.

Dating from his return to Florence that same year, Piero's fortunes began to fail. By 1475 his finances were so precarious he appealed to Lorenzo to help him, citing the Medici family friendship with Simonetta. Lorenzo was not

Madonna della misericordia
Domenico Ghirlandaio with brother David
(circa 1472)
detached fresco
Vespucci Chapel, Church of Ognissanti
Florence
(The Madonna of Mercy is reputed to be
the portrait of Simonetta protecting the
Vespucci family. Immediately to the left of
her figure is the alleged portrait of
Amerigo Vespucci.)

sympathetic. After the death of Simonetta, Piero turned to the Pazzi with his supplications and loyalties. Thus, he was considered a part of the Pazzi conspiracy.

After Piero was jailed for his part in the conspiracy, he appealed to Lucrezia de' Medici, reminding her of the gentleness their family had shown to Giuliano after Simonetta's death. Lucrezia implored Lorenzo to grant the Vespucci family a pardon. In 1480, Lorenzo reluctantly released Piero from jail. He then exiled the family to Milan. There Piero was killed in an insurrection in 1485.

Marco Vespucci- 1453-1497

One year after the death of Simonetta, Marco Vespucci married Costanza de Rechi Caponi. They had nine children, the male descendant line remaining until 1875 and the female line still existing today.

Marco remained a relatively unremarkable man. He was jailed along with his father for a short time after the Pazzi Conspiracy. During this period his family was indigent. He, as well as his father, wrote letters to Lucrezia de' Medici begging forgiveness from the Medici for his father and himself for their part in the conspiracy. Like his father, Marco was released in 1480 and exiled with his family.

In 1497, twelve years after his father was killed in an insurrection in Milan and three years after il Magnifico's death, Marco was killed during a brawl in the streets of Milan, leaving his family destitute.

Acknowledgments

There are three people to whom I owe my great appreciation and without whom this book would not exist. My husband, John, has been my "Napoleon's Corporal" as he likes to phrase it, throughout the writing of this book, keeping me well fed and editing on demand. Kathy Garvey is the "book mother" in every sense of the word. She has encouraged and supported me in addition to providing technical and editorial expertise throughout the more than two year writing process. Her skill and patience in designing and editing the book has made its publication possible. Finally, the extraordinary scholarship of Rachele Farina in her book, *Simonetta: Una donna alla corte dei Medici* has provided invaluable information.

The careful reading and astute editorial comments of Denette Schweikert and David Richardson have immeasurably improved the final outcome of my efforts. Many thanks go to them for the time and effort they have expended. Thanks also go to my dear friends, Hadwig and Walter Herrmann. Hadwig was kind enough to give me the latest published work on Simonetta, *Botticellis Idealportraits der Simonetta Vespucci* by Daniela Venner and to translate it for me from the German into French. Walter relinquished his long treasured article from *The Observer* on Lorenzo de'Medici. I would also like to thank Cindy Michaud, Claire Peffer and Hila Richardson who read and provided valuable feedback on the manuscript in progress.

In addition, I want to recognize two Italian acquaintances who have helped me in my pursuit of Simonetta's story. Marco Ferritti, my Italian instructor at the Koine Center in Florence, was the first to introduce me to the "real" Simonetta. He also recommended Rachele Farina's book which had just been published. Signora Delfina Scalzitti currently with The Boboli Gardens graciously obtained permission for me to do research on Botticelli in the Biblioteche Ufizzi, a unique and unforgettable experience.

I would like to acknowledge those who have supported and encouraged me in my many endeavors: my friends and former colleagues, Ron Maney, Melanie Biermann, Barbara Ottinger, and Gillian Ahlgren; and the members of the Pieces of Eight art group and the Cindy Babich Book Club. To my daughters, Lisa Picardi and Gianna Kennedy, and to my grandchildren, Jack, Madeline, Will and Mac Kennedy, I owe unending gratitude for filling my days with life, laughter and love.

Art Notes

The following paintings of Sandro Botticelli are referred to or used for descriptions in the narrative of *Simonetta*.

p. 25   *The Birth of Venus,* tempera on canvas. 1484. Florence, Galleria degli Uffizi. Painting on wedding chest.

p. 26   *Venus and Mars,* tempera on panel. 1483. London, National Gallery. Simonetta's reverie.

p. 30   Background from The *Birth of Venus.* Cinque Terre.

p. 87   *Nastagio degli Oresti IV,* tempera on paper. 1483. Private Collection. Vespucci wedding feast.

p. 135   *Venus and Mars.* Pearl and garnet brooch.

p. 135   *The Primavera,* tempera on panel. 1481-1482. Florence, Galleria degli Uffizi.

p. 139   *Ideal Portrait of a Lady-Simonetta Vespucci,* tempera on poplar. 1475-1480. Frankfort am Main, Stadt Museum. Braids.

p. 142   *Adoration of the Magi,* tempera on panel. 1475. Florence, Galleria degli Uffizi.

p. 145   *The Portrait of a Man with Medal of Cosimo the Elder,* tempera on panel. 1475. Florence, Galleria degli Uffizi.

p. 145   *St. Augustine,* detached wall painting. 1480. Florence, Church of the Ognissanti.

p. 148   *Simonetta Vespucci,* drawing. 1476. Oxford, Ashmolean Museum. Study of face.

p. 151   *Ismarelda Bandinilli,* tempera on panel. 1475. London, Victoria and Albert Museum.

p. 152   *The Birth of Venus.* Botticelli's comment.

p. 216   *Giuliano de' Medici with Mourning Dove,* tempera on panel. 1478-1480. Washington, National Gallery of Art.

Bibliography

Primary Sources

Medici, Lorenzo de'. *Lorenzo de' Medici: Selected Poems and Prose*. Ed. Jon Thiem. Trans. Jon Thiem and Others. University Park, Pennsylvania: The Pennsylvania State University Press, 1991.

Tornabuoni, Lucrezia (de' Medici). *Sacred Narratives*. Trans. Jane Tylus. Chicago: The University of Chicago Press, 2001.

Secondary Sources

Arciniegas, German. *Le Monde de la Belle Simonetta*. Trans. Georges Lomne. France: Edition Espaces 34, 1998.

Arasse, Daniel. *Botticelli, de Laurent le Magnifique à Savonarole*. Luxembourg, Belgium: Skira, 2003.

Baldassarri, Stefano Ugo and Arielle Saiber, eds. *Images of Quattrocento Florence: Selected Writings in Literature, History and Art*. New Haven: Yale University Press, 2000.

Baldini, Umberto. *The Horne Museum: A Florentine House of the Renaissance*. Firenze: Edizioni della Meridiana, 2001.

Ballerini, Isabella Lapi. *The Medici Villas Complete Guide.* Firenze: Giunti, 2006.

Belozerskaya, Marina. *The Medici Giraffe: And Other Tales of Exotic Animals and Power.* New York: Little, Brown and Company, 2006.

Busignani, Alberto. *Botticelli.* Firenze, Italia: Sadea/Sandsoni Editori, 1965.

Casazza, Ornella. *Domenico Ghirlandaio: La Pittura.* Firenze: Giunti-Nardini Editore, 1983.

Cecchi, Alessandro. *Botticelli.* Milano, Italia: Fredrico Motta Editore, 2005.

Christiansen, Keith and Stefan Weppelmann, ed. *The Renaissance Portrait, From Donatello to Bollini.* New York: Metropolitan Museum of Art, 2012.

Cornini, Guido. *Botticelli.* Florence: Giunti, 2004.

Cross, Colin. "Lorenzo the Magnificent." *The Observer, May 11, 1969*: 11-30. Periodical.

Dempsey, Charles. *L'amour et la "Ninfa" chez Botticelli.* Luxembourg, Belgium: Skira, 2003.

Farina, Rachele. *Simonetta: Una donna alla corte de' Medici.* Torino: Bollati Boringhieri, 2001.

Freeman, Margaret B. *Herbs for the Medieval Household.* New York: The Metropolitan Museum of Art, 1997.

Graham, J.H. *Sandro Botticelli e la Rinascita di Simonetta Vespucci.* Arlington, Virginia : La Spezia, 1983.

Hagen, Rose-Marie and Rainer. *15th Century Paintings*. Italy: Taschen, 2001.

Hale, John R. *Renaissance*. New York: Time Life Books, 1971.

Horne, Herbert. *Sandro Botticelli*. London: G. Bell & Sons, 1908.

Lucas-Dubreton, Jean. *Daily Life in Florence: In the Time of the Medici*. Trans. A. Lytton Sells. New York: The Macmillan Company, 1961.

Martines, Lauro. *April Blood: Florence and the Plot against the Medici*. London: Pimlico, 2004.

Mateer, David, ed. *The Renaissance in Europe: Courts, Patrons and Poets*. New Haven: Yale Univerity Press, 2000.

Paolucci, Antonio. *Sandro Botticelli et la Puissance des Medicis*. Luxembourg, Belgium: Skira, 2003.

Pauli, Erika, trans. *Art and History of Florence*. Firenze: Bonechi. (No date.)

Plebani, Eleonora. *Lorenzo e Giuliano de' Medici: tra potere e legami di sangue*. Roma, Italia : Biblioteca di cultura / Bulzoni Editore, 1993.

Righini, Mariella. *Florentine*. France: Flammariin, 1995.

Rowdon, Maurice. *Lorenzo The Magnificent*. Chicago: Henry Regnery Company, 1974.

Ruzzante, Anne Ellis, trans. *Botticelli* (Art Classics). New York: Rizzoli, 2009.

Santi, Bruno. *Palazzo Medici Riccardi and the Benozzo Gozzoli Chapel.* Florence, Italy: Lo Studiolo, 1983.

The Medici Villa of Careggi. Florence: Azienda Opedaliere Universitaria Careggi. Pamphlet. (No date.)

The Wonders of Culture. Rome, Italy: Ministry for Cultural Heritage and Activities. Italy: MP Mirabilia Publications, 2006.

Trkulja, di Silvia Meloni. *I Cenacoli—Museo di Firenze.* Firenze: Becocci/Scala, 2002.

Unger, Miles J. *Magnifico: The Brillaint Life and Violent Times of Lorenzo de' Medici.* New York: Simon & Schuster, 2008.

Vannuci, Marcello. *Il magnifo racconta.* Roma, Italia: Newton Compton, 1991.

Venner, Daniela. *Botticellis Idealportraits der Simonetta Vespucci.* Saarbrucken, Germany: VDM Verlag Dr. Müller GmbH & Co., 2010.

Welch, Evelyn. *Art and Society in Italy:1350-1500.* New York: Oxford University Press, 1997.

Wirtz, Rolf C. *Art & Architecture of Florence.* Cologne: Konemann, 2000.

Websites Consulted

http://aneafiles.webs.com/glossary.html

http://www.archive.org/stream/
livesofearlymedi00rossuoft/
livesofearlymedi00rossuoft_djvu.txt

http://brunelleschi.imss.fi.it/itineraries/place/
MediciVillaAtCareggi.html

http://www.chateaudechantilly.com/

http://commons.wikimedia.org/wiki/File:Villa_medicea_
di_Careggi_2.JPG

http://www.elfinspell.com/MediciPoem.html

http://en.wikipedia.org/wiki/Architecture_of_Florence

http://en.wikipedia.org/wiki/Lives_of_the_Most_
Eminent_Painters,_Sculptors,_and_Architects

http://en.wikipedia.org/wiki/Republic_of_Florence

http://www.escholarship.org/

http://www.feedbooks.com/book/6373/stanze-per-la-
giostra-del-magnifico-giuliano-di-pietro-de-medici

http://www.florentine-persona.com/glossary.html

http://www.italia.it/en/travel-ideas/unesco-world-
heritage-sites/porto-venere-and-cinque-terre.html

http://it.wikipedia.org/wiki/Ospedale_vecchio_di_San_
Giovanni_di_Dio

254

http://www.larsdatter.com/beds.htm

http://www.letteratura.rai.it/articoli/lorenzo-de-medici-politico-e-poeta/1157/default.aspx

http://www.metmuseum.org/toah/hd/bifa/hd_bifa.htm

http://www.metmuseum.org/toah/works-of-art/25.30.22

http://www.museumsinflorence.com/index.html

http://www.nga.gov/content/ngaweb/Collection.html

http://www.nationalgallery.org.uk/paintings/

http://www.musee-conde.fr

http://www.museumsinflorence.com/musei/palazzo_davanzati.html

http://www.news.nationalgeographic.com/news/2014/02/140210-duomo-florence-brunelleschi-cathedral-architecture

http://www.oxfordbibliographies.com/view/document/obo-9780195399301/obo-9780195399301-0174.xml

http://www.palazzo-medici.it/mediateca/en/index.php? (Used extensively for archives, chronologies, pictures, inventories, descriptions.)

http://plato.stanford.edu/entries/ficino/

http://www.poderesantapia.com/engels/firenze/ognissanti.htm

http://www.psupress.org/books/SampleChapters/978-0-271-05641-8sc.html

http://www.wikiart.org/en/salvador-dali/after-the-head-of-giuliano-di-medici

http://www.wga.hu/html_m/b/botticel/7portrai/06medici.html

http://www.tesorodeimedici.it/index.php?en/58/places

http://www.thepinnaclelist.com/blog/2012/11/11/1806/portovenere-italy-hidden-treasure/1806/

http://thevespuccifamily.blogspot.com

http://www.virtualuffizi.com/botticelli-room.html

http://www.wga.hu/html_m/d/donatell/2_mature/various/window.html

Fay Picardi is an internationally published poet and Fulbright scholar whose volumes of poetry can be found on Amazon. *Simonetta* is the author's first prose work. In preparation for writing Simonetta's story, Fay spent months studying Italian, traveling throughout Tuscany and Liguria and doing research at the Biblioteca degli Uffizi and the Biblioteca Nationale di Firenze.

When she is not traveling, she lives in Florida with her husband.

Made in the USA
San Bernardino, CA
17 February 2019